ENCYCLOPAEDIA
OF
INDIAN GOVERNMENT:
PROGRAMMES AND POLICIES

Vol. 22

Law, Justice and Company Affairs

Edited by

Satish Tiwari

ANMOL PUBLICATIONS PVT. LTD.

NEW DELHI - 110 002 (INDIA)

ANMOL PUBLICATIONS PVT. LTD.
4374/4B, Ansari Road, Daryaganj
New Delhi - 110 002

Encyclopaedia of Indian Government: Programmes and Policies

First Edition, 2000
ISBN 81-261-0515-1 (Set)

PRINTED IN INDIA

Published by J.L. Kumar for Anmol Publications Pvt. Ltd., New Delhi - 110 002 and Printed at Mehra Offset Press, Delhi.

Contents

Preface

Encyclopaedia of Indian Government: Programmes and Policies contains authoritative information on about fifty departmental policies and their future developmental programmes.

Organised to be completed in 40 volumes, this gigantic work covers Agriculture; Atomic Energy; Chemicals and Fertilizers; Coal; Commerce; Communication; Culture; Defence; Education; Environment and Forests; External Affairs; Finance; Food & Consumer Affairs; Food Processing Industries; Health and Family Welfare; Home Affairs and Internal Security; Human Resources; Industry; Information and Broadcasting; Labour; Law, Justice and Company Affairs; Non-conventional Energy Sources; Ocean Development; Parliamentary Affairs; Personnel, Public Grievances and Pensions; Petroleum and Natural Gas; Planning and Programme Implementation; Planning and Statistics; Posts and Telegraphs; Power; Rural Development; Science and Technology; Social Justice and Empowerment; Space; States Affairs; Steel; Steel and Mines; Sugar and Edible Oils; Surface Transport; Textiles; Tourism; Urban Development; Water Resources; Women and Child development etc.

Based on the information derived from authoritative sources, this work contains authentic facts and figures. I am deeply beholden to all the scholars whose writings are cited or substantially made use of in the present work. I am also thankful to Anmol Publications Pvt. Ltd. for undertaking publication of this encyclopaedia. I am solely responsible for shortcomings in presentation of matter.

Encyclopaedic in nature, this will prove a dependable reference work for scholars and academics besides those appearing for different competitive examinations.

—**Satish Tiwari**

1

Department of Legal Affairs

Functions and organisation

The Department of Legal Affairs renders advice to the various Ministries/Departments of the Government of India on legal matters, carries out the conveyancing work of the Central Government and attends to the litigation work of the Central Government in die Supreme Court, High Courts, Tribunals and some of die subordinate Courts. It is also concerned with entering into treaties and agreements with foreign countries in matters of civil law, authorising officers to execute contracts and assurances of property on behalf of the President under article 299 (1) of the Constitution of India and signing and verifying of plaints and written statements in suits by or against the Union of India.

It is further concerned with the appointment of the Law Officers, namely, the Attorney-General for India, the Solicitor-General for India and Additional Solicitor General for India. Department of Legal Affairs administers the Advocates Act, 1961, the Notaries Act, 1952 and the Legal Services Authorities Act, 1987. This Department is also administratively incharge of Foreign Exchange Regulation Appellate Board, Income Tax Appellate Tribunal, Indian Legal Service and Law Commission of India.The Department has a two-tier organisational set up, namely, the Main Secretariat at New Delhi and the Branch Secretariats at Mumbai, Calcutta, Chennai and Bangalore.

Main secretariat

The set up at the Main Secretariat includes the Law Secretary, Additional Secretary, Legal Adviser (Conveyancing), Joint Secretary and Legal Advisers and other Legal Advisers at various levels. 'Me work relating to tendering of legal advice and conveyancing has been distributed amongst groups of officers. Each group is normally headed by a Joint Secretary and Legal Adviser who in turn is assisted by a number of officers at different levels.

The litigation work in the Supreme Court on behalf of all Ministries/Departments of the Government of India and some administrations of the Union territories is handled by the Central Agency Section presently headed by an Additional Secretary.

The litigation work in the Delhi High Court on behalf of the Ministries/Departments of the Government of India is processed by the High Court Litigation Section headed by an Additional Legal Adviser.

The litigation work in the subordinate courts in Delhi is handled by the Litigation (Lower Court) section headed by an Assistant Legal Adviser.

The Department has a special Cell dealing with implementation of the recommendations of the Law Commission and also with the legal profession and Administration of the Advocates Act, 1961.

One Joint Secretary level officer each, exclusively functions as Legal Adviser for Railway Board, Ministry of Commerce and Central Bureau of Investigation respectively. These Joint Secretaries also function from the above offices. Another Joint Secretary level officer acts exclusively as an Arbitrator under the Scheme of

Permanent Machinery of Arbitation, and functions from the office of the Bureau of Public Enterprises. In addition, officers of different levels, such as Additional Legal Adviser, Deputy Legal Adviser and Assistant Legal Adviser are posted in the Ministry of Agriculture, Ministry of Defence Ministry of Labour, Ministry of Urban Affairs and Employment and DGS&D.

Advice work

During the period from January, 1998 to 31st December, 1998, 9,682 written references for advice on various aspects of law were received from the various Ministries/ Departments/Offices of the Government of India. In addition, the Officers of this Ministry also participated in various international meetings and conferences. 147 Legislative proposals and other important matters were received for examination from legal and constitutional angles.

(i) 499 references relating to conveyancing including a number of international agreements and 30 references concerning House Building advances were dealt with.

(ii) Apart from tendering advice, the Department also handled notices received by the office of the Attorney, General of India, private parties, the Supreme Court of India, High Courts and other Courts as well as communications received by the Minister and other officers of this Ministry for consideration.

(iii) During the aforesaid period, 157 references relating to State Bills and Ordinances were received for examination from legal and constitutional angles.

(iv) About 252 meetings of Group of Ministers, Cabinet, Committee of Secretaries and other were attended by the officers of this Department. 17 meetings of' the committee on disputes covering 700 items were attended during the period under report. 48 Parliament questions, 16 private member's Bills and

16 international agreements relating to avoidance of double taxation and prevention of fiscal evasion with respect to taxes on income and bilateral investment, promotion and protection were also dealt with during this period.

(v) In the year 1999-99, 53 new cases on different subjects were sent for the opinion of the Attôrney General of India. Out of which 38 opinions were received and have been forwarded to the respective Ministries/ Department of the Government of India.

(vi) In addition to this, 13 cases were sent to the Solicitor General of India and 15 cases, weir sent to the Additional Solicitor General of India for opinion. All the opinions were received and forwarded to the concerned Ministries/Departments after approval of the competent authorities.

(vii) The work relating to the compilation of opinion of the law officers, in the Computer was taken up. Opinions of' the Law Officers upto the year 1990 are already fed in the computer and the opinions for the year 1991 are tinder process. 2,995, previous opinions, rendered by the officers in the advice side of this Department during the period 1960-1970 were taken up for review, out of which, 1,521 files were weeded out and the rest were marked for further retention.-

Association with statutory or quasi-judicial authorities

As a law member of the Tribunal set up in the Department of Mines under section 30 of the Mines and Minerals (Regulation and Development) Act, 1957, one Joint Secretary and Legal Adviser of this Department, disposed of 303 revision petitions.

Central agency section

The Central Agency Section (CAS), was set tip in the year 1950. It is presently headed by an Additional Secretary, who is assisted by a Senior Government Advocate, three

Deputy Government Advocates and six Assistant Government Advocates with usual complement of supporting, Gazetted and non-Gazetted staff.

The Section is responsible for the conduct of litigation work, in the Supreme Court on behalf of all Ministries/ Departments of the Central Government and some Administrations of the Union territories and also on behalf of the participating State Governments.

Government Advocates in the Central Agency Section are Advocates-on-record of the Supreme Court. They appear before the Supreme Court in all matters as per the Supreme Court Rules and whenever necessary, engage the Law Officers and Senior Counsels to lead them in the Court. They assist the Law Officers and other Advocates in the panel of Central Government Counsels.

The Counsels are paid fees prescribed by the Central Government. The fee bills of the Counsels are scrutinised and the fees payable is certified by the Government Advocates of the Central Agency Section.

During the period from 1.4.98 to 30.11.98, the Central Agency Section received 1,284 new cases from various Departments of the Government of India as well as the Union territories in which the Union of India or Union territories were either petitioners or respondents.

The programme of computerization in the Central Agency Section was vigorously pursued during the period under report. As part thereof, the National Informatics Centre (NIC) installed a Local Area Network (LAN). NIC has installed a 100 MHZ multiuser Pentium machine with 3 LAN Terminal Servers, through which 25 terminals 15 printers have been connected for providing terminal facility to the Government Advocates and various units in the Central Agency Section. These terminals will be used for updating the status of old and new cases and keeping .track of movement of files. A 386-system with 2 terminals is being used in the Record Room for feeding of data in respect of the available files pertaining to pending cases so as to make the CAS data-base upto-date.

NIC imparted training to 40 staff members of the Central Agency Section in updating and work processing for about 15 days.

In accordance with suggestion of the NIC, the CAS also procured leased data circuit line between the CAS, Supreme Court and NIC for providing NICNET connection at the CAS. The system has been recently made operational. The same will be used to send and receive E-Mail letters to and from various Ministries and Departments of the Government. This connection will also be used to access COURTNIC, JUDIS and INTERNET. The NICNET facilities will be available to all the Government Advocates and senior officials of the CAS.

The services of the one programmer from NIC have been procured on the part-time basis who is responsible for maintaining the software and hardware as well as for monitoring required modifications in the existing software or other necessary developments, pertaining to computerization of the CAS.

Litigation (higgh court) section

The litigation work in Delhi High Court and Central Administrative Tribunal. Principal Bench at New Delhi On behalf of all Ministries/Departments of the Government of India, except Railways and incometax Departments, is handled by the Litigation (High Court Section. The litigation work in the Delhi High Court and CAT is looked after by an Additional Legal Adviser assisted by an Assistant Legal Adviser. Cases dealt with, generally relate to Civil and Criminal Writ Petitions under Articles 226 and 227 of the Constitution of India, letters patent Appeals, Suits, Appeals, Reviews, Civil Revisions, Civil

Miscellaneous Applications, Division Bench Appeals, Company Applications, Execution Applications and Criminal Miscellaneous and Service matters.

There is a panel Of Central Government Standing Counsels and Government Counsels who are nominated for contesting the cases. In most important matters, Senior Counsels are engaged at the request of the Ministries/ Departments concerned. In some matters of public importance and also in complicated matters, one of the Law Officers, namely, Attorney-General for India, Solicitor-General of India or Additional Solicitors-General of India is also engaged. On receipt of request% from the Ministries/ Departments, action is taken for engaging a suitable counsel to appear on their behalf in the cases. Close liaison is maintained with various Departments Counsels to safeguard the interest of the Government in Litigation cases in the High Court at Delhi and CAT. The Additional Legal Advisers and other officers keep close watch over the progress of the cases at every stage.

Fee bills received from the Counsel are scrutinised having regard to the terms and conditions of their appointments before certifying for payments at the prescribed scales.

During the period from 1.1.98 to 30.11-98, Litigation (High Court) Section has engaged Counsel in 3,826 cases to safeguard the interest of the Government and to conduct litigation in Delhi High Court and Central Administrative Tribunal.

Litigation (lower court) section

During the period upto 30.11.1998, 350 new cases were received and 145 cases were disposed of by this section. At present, there are a total of 8,437 Court cases pending in various subordinate Courts/Tribunals in Delhi and New Delhi.

Judicial section

The Judicial Section is responsible for the Organisation of litigation of the Government of India and Union territories before the Supreme Court, various High Courts, the Central Administrative Tribunal and District anti subordinate Courts. Its functions include the processing of appointments of the Attorney General for India, the Solicitor-General and the Additional Solicitors-General of India, Central Government Counsel in the Supreme Court, High Courts, the Central Administrative Tribunals and District and Subordinate Courts and Consumer for a in some of the States, for conducting litigation work on behalf of the Central Government, engagement of Law Officers and other Counsels on behalf of Ministries/ Departments for the conduct of cases before the Supreme Court, High Courts, Tribunals, Commission of Inquiry, Districts and Subordinate Courts, Quasi-Judicial Authorities, etc. Its functions also include formulation and settlement of their terms and conditions for conducting cases.

The Judicial Section is responsible for nomination of Arbitrators in disputes between the various Departments of the Government of India and Private Parties as also in disputes involving the Union of India and Public Sector Undertakings or between such undertakings inter se. It appoints Counsel to appear in arbitration disputes between the CPWD, DGS&D or Ministry of Defence, etc., on the one hand and private contractors on the other.

It is also responsible for die administration of the Notaries Act, 1952 and the appointment of notaries. About 1,373 notaries appointed by the Central Government as on date are practising in various parts of the country. The section conducts enquiries into the allegations of professional or other misconduct on the part of the notaries.

It is further responsible for issuing statutory orders, e.g., orders under article 299 of the Constitution, authorising various officers to execute contracts for and on behalf of the President of India as also under Rule I of Order XXVII of Schedule I to the Code of Civil Procedure, 1908, authorising officers to sign and verify pleadings:

Implementation cell

The main functions of the Implementation cell is to process the report-, of the Law Commission for implementation in consultation with the Ministries/ Departments concerned. The cell is also concerned with the administration of the Advocates Act, legal education and legal profession.

The 14th Law Commission under the chairmanship of Shri Justice K.J. Reddy submitted the 156th Report on the Indian Penal Code which have been laid on 8th and 9th June, 1998 on the tables of Lok Sabha and Rajya Sabha respectively. 15th Law Commission under the Chairmanship of Shri Justice B.P. Jeevan Reddy have submitted 157th Report on "Section 52: transfer of Property Act and its amendments". 158th Report- on "The Amendments of the Industries (Development and Regulation) Act, 1951", 159th Report on "Repeal and Amendment of Laws: Part-I". 160th Report on "Amendment to the All India Council for Technical Education, Act 1987 (Act No. 52 of 1987)". 161st Report on "Central Vigilance Commission and Allied Bodies", 1622nd Report on "Review of functioning of Central Administrative Tribunal, CEGAT and ITAT", 163rd Report on "The Code of Civil Procedure (Amendment) Bill, 1997", 164th Report on "The Indian Divorce Act (IV o 1869)" and 165th Report on "Free and Compulsory Education for Children" during 1998 which are yet to he laid in the Parliament.

National legal service authority

The Government, of India is committed to give Legal Aid to the poor in as much as equality before law is a constitutional promise. Article 39A of the Constitution of India enjoins upon the Government to provide legal aid to the poor and weaker sections of the society to ensure equal justice for all, the cardinal principle on which the administration of justice is based. It is said that nothing rankles mote in the human heart than a brooding- sense of injustice. The pursuit of justice by the poor is compounded by their illiteracy and ignorance and as such it is for the State to focus its attention on legal aid, legal literacy and legal awareness programmes with multi dimensional strategies to infuse confidence anti courage in the masses to wage a legal battle against every injustice and oppression. The Legal Services Authorities Act, 1987 is an apt tribute to the framers of our Constitution who had dreamed of a society in which (here would be political, social and economic equality to every citizen. The Act aims at establishing a nation-wide network for providing free and competent legal services to the weaker sections of the society on the basis of equal opportunity. National Legal Services Authority (NALSA) has been set up to monitor and oversee the legal aid programmes throughout the country. In every State a State Legal Services Authority has to be set up for implementing the legal aid programmes in that State. At District and Taluk levels also legal Services Authorities/Committees are being established to ensure that Legal Services are easily available even to the poorest amongst the poor throughout the country. The Supreme Court Legal Service Committee has been constituted under the Act for giving legal aid in the matters coining before Supreme Court of India. In every High Court also, the High Court Legal Services Committees are being established to provide free legal aid to the eligible persons in the legal matters coming before the High Courts.

The provisions of Chapter III of the Legal Services Authorities Act have now been extended to all States and Union territories. They have already finalised, and notifies State Legal Services Authorities Rules in their respective State Gazettes for the Constitution of State Legal Services Authorities. National Legal Services Authorities having its office at New Delhi is headed by the Chief Justice of India, who is the ex-officio Patron-in-Chief. Hon'ble Mr. Justice S.P. Barucha, the senior-most Judge of the Supreme Court of India is the present Executive Chairman of the Authority. The Central Authority constituted vender Section 3 of the Legal Services Authorities Act is taking necessary steps to establish vibrant legal aid network in the country, and is formulating policies, principles and schemes to achieve the aims and objects of the Act. A grants-in-aid of Rupees four crores has been sanctioned by the Central Government for NALSA, so that it may allocate appropriate funds to the State and District authorities and also provide grants-in-aid for specific schemes to various voluntary social services institutions and State as well as District Authorities. NALSA is also monitoring and evaluating the implementation of the legal aid programmes in the country and is taking appropriate measures for spreading legal literacy and legal awareness amongst the weaker sections of the society.

Admissibility for legal aid

Under the Act, free legal services are admissible to every citizen whose income is less than Rs. 9,000/ per annum in cases before subordinate courts and High Courts and Rs. 12,000/- per annum in cases before the Supreme Court. The State Government can, however, fix higher income limits. The means test is, however, not applicable in the case of persons belonging to the Scheduled Castes, Scheduled Tribes, women, children and handicapped. At the first annual meet of the Legal Services Authorities held under the aegis of the NALSA on 12th September, 1998 in New Delhi, it was unanimously resolved that for cases before High Courts, the minimum income ceiling in every State should be raised to Rs. 25,000/- per annum and for the cases before the Supreme Court of India it should be raised to Rs. 50.0001- per annum.

Achivements

According to the information available with NALSA as on 31st December, 1998, about 25,600 Lok Adalats have been held in different parts of the country where about 80.38 lakhs cases were settled. In about 4,16,000 motor vehicles accident claims cases, compensation amounting to over Rs. 1,591 crores was awarded.

Steps are also being taken to provide special legal aid facilities to women prisoners in jail to ensure that (he right of an undertrail to have interview with his counsel is not denied, to appoint legal aid counsels in the courts of Magistrates, to set up Legal Aid Clinics in Law Colleges and Universities, etc.

Branch secretariat, Mumbai

The Branch Secretariat at Mumbai is headed by a Joint Secretary and Legal Adviser who is assisted by one Senior Central Government Advocate, one Additional Legal Adviser, four Central Government Advocates, two Deputy Legal Advisers, two Assistant Legal Advisers and other supporting staff.

Functions of the Branch Secretariat are carried out by three Sections, viz., Advice, Litigation and Administration. The Advice Section mainly deals with advising the various Departments of Government of India on all legal matters. It is also concerned with conveyancing work of the Central Government offices which come under its purview.

The Litigation Section is responsible for the conduct of Litigation work in the Mumbai High Court for various Departments of Government of India through their Panel

Counsels, except cases of railways. Panel Counsel consist of special Senior Grade 1, Senior Grade 11 and Junior Counsels who appear before the High Court and plead on behalf of the Government of India. There exists a separate panel for Income-tax matters. These counsels are briefed by Branch Secretariat, keeping in view the value and importance of cases. In important matters, Law officers and Special Counsels of the panel are engaged. 'Mere is one Additional Solicitor General for Mumbai High Court, who also helps in varying out litigation work more effectively.

With a view to exercising effective control over litigation work in the High Court of Gujarat, Madhya Pradesh, Rajasthan and also Nagpur, Goa and Aurangabad Branches of the Mumbai High Court and for ensuring better coordination between Central Government Departments, on the one hand and the Standing Counsel in these courts on the other, the joint Secretary and Legal Adviser supervises the litigation work pertaining to Central Government offices in these courts by personal visits to these places, holding discussions with the' concerned Department, Officers and Counsel.

The Mumbai Branch Secretariat also exercises general supervision over litigation work in subordinate courts in Mumbai. The Branch Secretariat also looks after service cases relating to Central Government employees before die Central Administrative Tribunal (CAT), Mumbai through the Panel Counsels.

Joint Secretary and Legal Adviser was appointed as the sole Arbitrator for settling disputes between Government Departments, Public Sector Undertakings and Private Parties and he has given several awards in such disputes.

The Memo of fee received from the various standing

panel counsels engaged to appear on behalf of the Central Government in the Mumbai High Court are scrutinised and proper fees is certified by the Central Government Advocates concerned and sanctioned by the Joint Secretary and Legal Adviser and paid through cheques; out of die funds allotted. The fee bills of Standing Counsels of other High Courts and subordinate courts within die jurisdiction of this Branch Secretariat are also exammed and certified by the Joint Secretary arid Legal Adviser for payment by the Department concerned.

During the current year, the work relating to computerisation of the Branch Secretariat has been done with a separate computer room being set up and six computer terminals installed in it.

Branch secretariat, Calcutta

The Branch Secretariat at Calcutta is headed by a Joint Secretary and Legal Adviser. It has six wings viz. Advice, Administration, Cash and Accounts, Hindi, Counsel Fee Bill and Litigation Section. The litigation section of this Branch Sectt. Looks after the Calcutta High Court litigation cases both in the Original and Appellate Side and its Circuit Bench at Port Blair.

The Branch Secretariat is responsible for conducting litigation cases in all the courts within its jurisdiction with a view to control over litigation works in the High Court- The Advice Section of this Branch Secretariat holds discussions with the concerned departmental officers and Counsels. The Branch Secretariat also exercises general supervision over litigation work in subordinate courts within its jurisdiction. The Branch Secretariat also looks after service matters relating to Central Government employees before the. Central Administrative Tribunal, Calcutta Bench through its Advice Section and also supervises the other similar litigation matter in other Benches of the Central Administrative Tribunal situated in its jurisdiction. The Branch Secretariat furnishes legal advice and also conducts litigation cases of all the Central Government Departments including Ministry of Finance and its Departments eg. Income-tax Department, Customs and Central Excise, Revenue Intelligence, FERA, Ministry of Railways, Ministry of Defence and all other Departments located in the Eastern Region of the country i.e. West Bengal, Assam, Nagaland, Manipur, Arunachal Pradesh, Meghalaya, Bihar, Orissa including Union territory of Andaman and Nicobar Administration.

The Advice side is under the charge of the Joint Secretary and Legal Adviser who is assisted by one Deputy Legal Adviser. This Branch Secretariat gives legal opinion to the offices of the Central Government regarding Constitution, Arbitration, Service, and Land Acquisition matters. Conduct of Arbitration cases on behalf of Central Government and vetting and finalisation of pleadings. Affidavits, etc., are also looked after by the Advice Wing of the Branch Secretariat. The total number of cases disposed of by the Advice Wing up to November, 1998 is 2311 and it is expected that the cases to be handled during the 1998-99 will be around 3500.

Conveyancing work i.e. finalisation of documents and agreements entered into between different department-, of the Central Government in the Eastern Region and Private Parties or Semi-Government institutions are approved and vetted by this Branch Secretariat.

The Litigation work include conducting of cases on behalf of the Central Govt. in the Original side and Appellate side through a panel of Counsels. Pleadings filed in various Courts as well as Central Administrative Tribunals am also vetted by this Branch Secretariat. Senior Central Government Advocate, Central Government Advocate and Junior Central Government Advocate look after the litigation side of the Calcutta High Court and sometimes they are also required to appear before the Court in miscellaneous matters and petition for special leave to appeal. Depending upon the exigencies of work, sometimes the advocates are also required to appear in regular appeals and Writ Petitions. The total number of cases handled by the litigation Division is 1246 till November, 1998 and the number of cases expected to be handled during 1998-99 will be around 1900. Similarly, around 800 CAT cases are expected to be handled during 1.99899.

Professional Fee Bills of Counsels for litigation in the Courts engaged by the Ministry of Law and justice for Central Government litigations in the Calcutta High Court are paid by this Branch Secretariat. Such payments during the financial year is expected to be around Rs. 38,00,000/-.

The Branch Secretariat also certified professional bills of the counsels forwarded by the different Departments and Ministries of the Central Government which are finally paid by such departments.

A computer system has been installed in the Branch Secretariat Calcutta in 1998 by NIC and the same is being fully used by the staff of this office. This system has been of special help to litigation and Cash & Accounts work in addition to other routine work done by the Administration.

Branch secretariat, Chennai

The Branch Secretariat at Chennai is headed by a Deputy Legal Adviser.

Advice: The Branch Secretariat renders legal advices to all Central Government offices located in the State of Kerala, Tamil Nadu and the Union territory of Pondicherry. During the period from 1-4-1998 to 3011-1998, about 2689 references for advice were dealt with. In the absence of

Head of Office for Branch Secretariat Bangalore, the Head of Office of the Branch Secretariat, Chennai also looked after the work of Branch Secretariat Bangalore, whenever such occasion arose.

Litigation: The Branch Secretariat looks after the entire litigation work of the Central Government (except relating to Railways and Incometax) in the High Court of Kerala and the High Court of Madras, in the City Civil Courts and the Presidency Court of Small Causes, in the Ernakulam and the Chennai Benches of the Central Administrative Tribunal and in some other Tribunals. The Branch Secretariat has also been entrusted with the work of Central Government litigation in the District Consumer Disputes Redressal Forum and the State Consumer Redressal Commission, both at Chennai.

The Branch Secretariat keeps the Ministries/ Departments of the Central Government informed about the important developments of their cases as well as the results of the litigation, with suitable advice for further action, if required, pleading, affidavits, etc., to be filed in the Courts/Tribunals/Consumer Fora/Arbitration matters in Tamil Nadu and Kerala are scrutinised and vetted at the draft stage. Documents furnished by the litigant departments are examined before filing or producing them in the Courts. The officers from this Branch Secretariat also brief the Counsel at every stage of the cases in the Courts. Functions also include engagement of the Counsel and collection of material from the Central Government departments involved in the cases, for being passed on to the Counsel, after necessary scrutiny of the documents from the legal angle.

The Government has appointed an Additional Solicitor General for Madras High Court since February, 1997.

Counsel fee bilis: The Branch Secretariat itself pays the fee directly from its centralised funds to the Senior Counsel and the Central Government Standing Counsels in the Madras High Court cases. Fee Bills preferred by an Additional Central Government Standing Counsel for appearance before the Central Administrative Tribunal, Chennai and Subordinate Courts at Chennai are scrutinised and certified and sent to the Departments concerned after certification for payment.

Branch secretariat, Banngalore

Branch Secretariat at Bangalore was set up in 1983 and renders legal advice to various Central Government Departments and offices located in the States of Karnataka and Andhra Pradesh. During the current year, i.e., 1998-99, as on 30-11-1998 about 5,725 references were received for advice. The advice work includes vetting of contracts, scrutiny and vetting of pleadings and counter affidavits to be filed in the Court/CAT, examination of the feasibility of filing appeals/review, etc., interpretation of laws, guidance to Departments on legal sustainability of their actions and holding discussion with the administrative Department, whenever necessary.

The Branch Secretariat supervises the entire litigation of the Central Government Departments and offices in the High Courts of Karnataka and Andhra Pradesh, subordinate courts of Bangalore city and twin cities of Hyderabad and Secunderabad and Central Administrative Tribunal in both the States. This

Secretariat also looks after the work of Government litigation in the District Consumer, Redressal Fora and the State Consumer Redressal Commission of both the States. 'Me functions of the Branch Secretariat in this regard include distribution of work among the Government Counsels, processing and payment of fees to Counsels in the Karnataka High Court, certification for payment of fee bills of the government counsels in the CAT/Subordinate Courts in Karnataka and all courts in Andhara Pradesh and maintaining liaison between the Government Departments situated outsidc Bangalore and die Courts.

Law cowhission of India

The 15th Law Commission has been reconstituted with effect from 1st September, 1997 for a period of three years ending on 31st August, 2000. Besides the Member-Secretary, Dr. S.C. Jain, who is of die rank of Secretary to the Government of India in the Ministry of Law, Justice & Company Affairs, the Commission comprises of the following:-.

Hon'ble Mr. Justice B.P. Jeevan Reddy (Retd.)- Chairman

Hon'ble Mrs. Justice Leila Seth (Retd.)- Member

Dr. N. M. Ghatate- Member

Dr. N.R. Madhava Menon-Part time Member

The terms of reference of the 15th Law Commission are as under:

I. Review/Repeal of obsolete laws:

(a) To identify laws which are no longer needed or relevant and can be immediately repealed:

(b) To identify laws which are in harmony with the existing climate of economic liberalization which need no change;

(c) To identify laws which require changes or amendments and to make suggestions for their amendment;

(d) To consider in a wider perspective the suggestions for revision/amendment given by Expert Groups in various Ministries/ Departments with a view to coordinating and harmonising them;

(e) To consider references made to it by Ministries/ Departments in respect of legislation having bearing on the working of more than one Ministry/Department;

(f) To suggest suitable measures for quick redressal of citizens grievances, in the field of law.

II. Law and Poverty

(a) to examine the laws which affect the poor and carry (nit post-audit for socio-economic legislation.

(b) to take all such measures as may be necessary to harness law and the legal process in the service of the poor.

III. To keep under review the system of judicial administration to ensure that it is responsive to the reasonable demands of the times and in particular to secure:

(a) elimination of delays, speedy clearance of arrears and reduction of costs so as to secure quick and economical disposal of cases without affecting the cardinal principle that decisions should be just and fair.

(b) simplification of procedure to reduce and eliminate technicalities and devices for delay so that it operates not as an end in itself but as a means of achieving justice.

(c) improvement of standards of all concerned with the administration of justice.

IV. To examine the existing laws in the light of Directive Principles of State Policy and to suggest ways of improvement and reform and also to suggest such legislation as might be necessary to implement the Directive Principles and to attain the objective set out in the Preamble to the constitution.

V. To revise, the Central Acts of general importance so as to simplify them and to remove anomalies, ambiguities and inequities.

VI. To recommend to the Government measures for bringing the statute book-up-to-date by repealing obsolete laws and enactments or parts thereof which have outlived their utility.

VII. To consider and to convey to the Government its views on any other subject relating to law and judicial administration that may be referred to it.

The Commission took up various subjects indicated in its terms of reference. A questionnaire on the proposed amendments to the "Hire Purchase Act, 1972", working papers respectively on "Reform, of the Electoral Laws" and "Legislation to Forfeit Property of Corrupt Public Servants" were issued to elicit views/suggestions on these subjects from the various concerned persons/organisations including Government agencies. 'Me 15th Law Commission has submitted the following reports:

(a) 157th report on "Section 52: Transfer of Property Act, 1882 and its amendment";

(b) 158th report on "The Amendment of the Industries (Development and Regulation) Act, 195 1 ";

(c) 159th report on "Repeal and Amendment of Laws: Part-I";

(d) 160th report on "Amendment to the All India Council for Technical Education Act, 1987 (52 of 1987)";

(e) 161st report on "Central Vigilance Commission and Allied Bodies;

(f) 162nd report on "Review of Functioning of Central Administrative Tribunal, Customs, Excise and Gold (Control) Appellate Tribunal and incometax Appellate Tribunal";

(g) 163rd report on "The Code of Civil Procedure (Amendment) Bill, 1987";

(h) 164th report on "The Indian Divorce Act (IV of 1869)"; and

(i) 165th report on "Free and Compulsory Education for Children".

The Commission also organised press briefings inviting media to disseminate the information pertaining to the working papers released by the commission so that interested persons may send their views on them. In the press briefings, the Commission released a working paper on "Reform in Electoral LAW", and another working paper proposing "Legislation to Forfeit Property of Public Servants Possessing illegally acquired Properties", respectively.

The Commission held a seminar on Reforms in Electoral Law at India International Centre, New Delhi on 14-11-1998, inviting political parties, MPs. eminent media persons, academicians, etc., to present their views on the subject.

The Law Commission has also held jointly with the Bar Council of India, a National Seminar on Reforms in Electoral Laws at Vigyan Bhawan, New Delhi on 23rd and 24th January, 1999. It was inaugurated by the Hon'ble Prime Ministry of India, Shri Atal Behari Vajpayee.

Income-tax appellate tribunal

The Income tax Appellate Tribunal, constituted under the Income-tax Act, deals with second appeals in all matters relating to direct taxes, and appeals against orders of revision or Commissioners as well as orders of acquisition of properties under Chapter XXA of the Income-tax Act. At present there air 53 Benches of the Tribunal spread over 24 cities. The Tribunal is headed by a President who is assisted by one Senior Vice President and three Vice-

Presidents. The Tribunal consists of Judicial Members and Accountant Members. 'Me sanctioned strength of (he Members of the tribunal is 106. An Appeal lies to the High Court from the order of the Tribunal passed on or after 1. 10. 1998.

Generally, appeals are heard by a Bench consisting of one Accountant Member and one Judicial Member. However in appropriate Cases, a Bench may consist of more than two Members and where the taxable income is Rs. one lakh or less, they are disposed of even by a single Member Bench. For this purpose, the Government has empowered some of the senior members of the Tribunal to constitute Single Member Benches.

At the beginning of the 1998, the number of cases pending before the Tribunal was 3,00,333, and as on 1st November, 1998, the number of pending cases stood at 3,02,410. The pendency level is expected to come down with the new Benches becoming functional. Steps are also being taken to computerise office records and working procedure in Income-tax Appellate Tribunal. In pursuance of amendments made by the Finance Act, 1998, the fee structure in the Tribunal has been revised.

During the period under review, steps for implementation of the Official Languages Act, 1963 have been pursued vigorously. The progressive use of Hindi in day-to-day functioning has been further accelerated. Documents drawn up in Hindi can be presented in the Benches located in Hindi speaking States, at the Benches located in the States of Gujarat, Maharashtra, the Union territory of Chandigarh and the National Capital territory of Delhi, proceedings before the Tribunal may also be in Hindi and it is permissible to pass orders also in Hindi. However, where an order is passed in Hindi, it is to be accompanied by an authorised English translation.

To promote the use of Hindi in administration work,

an incentive scheme for preparing notes and drafts in Hindi has been introduced in all the Benches of the Tribunal. Attractive prizes have also been provided for this purpose

Official Languages Implementation committees have been constituted at all the Benches of the Tribunal to monitor the progress of achievements.

Mumbai Bench of the Tribunal has won appreciation for doing maximum work in Hindi during the period under Report.

Foreign exchangge regulation appellate board

The Foreign Exchange Regulation Appellate Board was established under the provisions of die Foreign Exchange Regulation Act, 1947. It has been continued -tinder the foreign Exchange Regulation Act, 1973 which repealed the 1947 Act. Under the Act, the Board is to comprise a Chairman and not more than four members. The sanctioned strength of the Board is a Chairman, one full time member and three part-time members. However, during the period the Board was comprised of the Chairman and two part-time Members as the post of full-time member remained vacant,

The Board has all India jurisdiction with its seat at New Delhi. It goes in circuit to hear appeals at places other than Delhi.

The Board hears appeals against the Adjudication Orders under which monetary penalties are imposed by the adjudicating authorities of the Enforcement Directorate for contravention of the provisions of the Act. The Board also has the power to suo moto call for the records of the adjudication proceedings for examining the legality, propriety or correctness of any order made by adjudicating authorities and pass appropriate order thereon.

During the period from 1-4-1998 to 1-12-1998, 148 appeals were filed. Total number of appeals disposed of from 1.1.1998 to 15.12.1998 is 72. The total disposal of interim application during the period i.e. 1-1-1998 to till date is 295.

Grants-in-aid to private organisations for legal research

With a view to promoting studies and research in matters of law, the Department of Legal Affairs sanctions grants-in-aid to certain institutions engaged in research in the field of law.

The India IAW institute

I. Publications released

(a) Journal of the Indian Law Institute

(i) Volume 38 No. 2 (April-June, 1996)

(ii) Volume 38 No. 3 (July-September, 1996)

(iii) Volume 38 No. 4 (Oct.-December, 1996)

(iv) Volume 39 No. I (January-March, 1997)

(b) Annual Survey of Indian Law, 1995

(c) 1994 Index to Journal of Indian Law Institute 1995 Index to, Journal of Indian Law Institute.

II. Research Projects

Project of the Ministry of Civil Supplies: Present project on the Indian Contract Act, the Sale of a Goods Act, the prevention of Adulteration Act: the 'Drugs & Magic Remedies Objectionable Advertisement Act) from the point of consumer, etc., is under study on behalf of the Ministry of Civil Supplies, Government of India. Work on this Project is still going on.

Research Project of the Ministry of Environment and Forest, Government of India.

In this regard a National workshop was held on the ,heme "Legal Regulation of Hazardous Substances and

Processes" from 29th to 1st December, 1997. The project report has been submitted to the Ministry.

Directory of Law Colleges in India: This is almost complete.

Fifty years of the Supreme Court:

A blue print for the proposed project on Fifty Years of the Supreme Court is being prepared.

III. Diploma Courses

The Institute continues to conduct the following Diploma courses:

1. Administrative Law
2. Corporate Laws & Management
3. Labour Law
4. Tax Laws

The examinations of Diploma courses for the session 1997-98 were held in May 1998.

Session for the year 1998-99 has already started.

IV. Diploma Course in Environment Law

Admission to this Diploma Course is under process.

V. M.B.A in Justice Administration

The Institute started the MBA course in Justice Administration in collaboration with the Edith Cowan University, Perth (Western Australia) in the year, 1995. The last examination was held on 15.6.1998 as scheduled.

VI. First Refresher Course in Law under UGC Scheme

The Institute organised the First UGC's sponsored Refresher Course in Law for Law Teachers in the areas of Environment Laws, Consumer protection Laws and Labour Laws from 14th December, 1998 to 2nd January, 1999. Thirty-three law Teachers from different Universities in India attended. Certificates were issued to !he Participants on 2.1.1999.

VII. Affiliation

Dr. K.P. Singh's affiliation continued with the Institute on sponsorship by the Indian Council of Social Science Research to conduct research on Socio-legal Impact on Tehri Dam Project on Local People.

Prof. Z. M. Shahid Siddiqui has been affiliated with the Indian Law Institute as an Emeritus Follow of the UGC with effect from 20.11.1998.

VIII. Visits by Scholars

A Professor and 63 students of Hooghly Mohsin College visited the Institute on 14.9.1998. They were addressed by Hon'ble Mr. Justice N.C. Kochhar, Former Hony. Director, ILI.

Mr. Hazaime Sato, IDE, JETRO, Japan visited the Institute on 28.10.1998 and exchanged the views with the Director, Prof (Ms.) S.K. Verma.

Professor R.A. Nakade and Mr. Shailesh R. Deshmukh alongwith 23 law students of Bharati Vidyapeeth, Pune visited the Institute on 3.12.1998. They were addressed by Professor Ms. S.K. Verma, Director of the Institute.

IX. Discussion/Dialogue

The Institute organised a Penal Discussion on "Article 3567- Mommai and After" on 30.10.1998.

Sh. B. Sen, Senior Advocate, Supreme Court of India presided.

Shri S.C. Sharma, Central Ground Water Board, Ministry of Water Resources, Government of India visited the Institute in November, 1998. A dialogue took place in respect of framing the detailed guidelines on various aspects.

Future programmes (from 1.1.1999 to 3331.3.1999)

The Institute plans to organise the following programme.% in the first quarter of the year:

UGC's sponsored Second Refresher Course, in Law for Law Teachers from different Universities in India from 8th March, to 27th March, 1999 followed by now i 'the next financial year.

Refresher Course's for the Judicial Officers in collaboration with the National Judicial Academy.

Next Sulakhana Devi Memorial Lecture.

New Certificate and Diploma Courses in:

(i) Environment Law

(ii) Inteliectual Property Law

(iii) Human rights

(iv) Commercial and Business Law

Project on "Fifty Years of the Supreme Court" (A blue print for this project is being prepared).

Publication of "Directory of Law Colleges/Law Teachers."

Publication of the following:

(i) Volume 39 No. 2-4 (April - December, 1997) of the Journal of Indian Law Institute.

(ii) Index to Journal of the Indian Law Institute (1996).

Revision of following research publications:

(a) Research Methodology

(b) State and Services Law

(c) Release on Bail

(d) Labour Law and Labour Relations: Cases and Materials

Digest of Judgments on Environment Law

Panel Discussion of the 3rd Judges Cases.

Panel Discussion on Rape and Capital Punishment.

Workshop in collaboration with the World Intellectual Property Organization, Geneva.

Research Project on Health Legislations Medical Ethics.

Seminar on electoral Reforms.

The Institute is in negotiation with Delhi Commission for Women to undertake a research study on Discrimination and Atrocities Against Women with special reference to rape and molestation in Delhi. The proposal has already been sent to the Commission on 26.10.1998.

A meeting was held with the Sri Lankan delegation consisting of the following on 4.1.1999:

(i) Dr. Jayampathi Wickremaratne, Consultant/Ministry of Justice, Constitutional Affairs, Ethic Affairs and National Integration and Member/Drafting Committee on the new Constitution.

(ii) Mr. Karunaratne Paranawithana, Assistant Secretary/ Ministry of Justice, Constitutional Affairs, Ethic Affairs and National Integration.

(iii) Mr. Nishan Muthukrishna, Project Director and Member/Drafting Committee on the new Constitution.

A lecture was delivered on 6.1.1999 by his excellency, Dr. Dullah Omar, South African Minister of Justice on the theme "Transportation of Justice System in South Africa".

To bring out 1,996 issue of the Annual Survey of Indian Law.

To bring out a Joint issue of 1997 and 1998 of die Annual Survey of Indian Law.

The institute of Constitutional nd parliamentary studies

(i) 31st Session

A few lectures and meetings were arranged for the benefit

or course participants during the concluding months of April and May, 1998.

Written examinations for the two diploma courses were held and viva voce was also held towards the end of the programme for screening the performance of (he parliamentary fellows as also the diploma students for the award of fellowships and certificates. The diploma students prepared some 21 research papers which were also included and evaluated for the award of certificates to them.

The parliamentary fellows visited states and part of the programme to acquaint themselves with the functioning of democracy at the state level and to enable them to see for themselves the different aspects of our life and people.

The 31st session concluded on 8th May, 1998 with the distribution of fellowships and diploma certificates at a simle ceremony by Hon'ble Shri Ram Niwas Mirdha, former Union Minister. The function was attended by the Members of the Executive Council and others.

(ii) 32nd Session:

After the successful completion of the 31st session, preparations for the 32nd session of the course were taken in hand. Forms and fact-sheets giving details regarding the course contents were prepared for the benefit of the prospective participants. This was followed by communications addressed to our missions abroad and foreign missions based at Delhi for the benefit of foreign participants particularly from Commonwealth countries who have been sponsoring candidates to the programme during the last three decades. The programme was also given wider publicity within the country by addressing letters to parliament/ legislatures, Bar Councils, universities, courts, union and state ministries. To provide wider publicity to the programme it was also advertised in the national dailies during the month of October, for information of the prospective candidates and sponsoring authorities. The programme commenced in the month of December with some 12 participants from within the country while five applications from Commonwealth countries (two each from Sri Lankan and Bangladesh and one from Swaziland) are yet to join. The Commonwealth secretariat, London has been requested to release funds for the nominees of the above mentioned Parliaments and the Institute is awaiting their original applications duly forwarded by the Commonwealth contact points of the sponsoring countries.

A detailed programme of lectures is being chalked out for the benefit of the participants. Preparations for branch-in-training in the two Secretaries of Parliament, government/ministries and other institutions are in hand.

(iii) Lectures, Discussions, etc:

During the period under report a few lectures were arranged for the course participants, members of the Institute and staff on topics related to constitutional law, parliamentary processes, etc.

(iv) G.V. Mavalankar Memorial Lecture:

Shri R. Venkataraman, former President of India on 7th December, 1998 delivered and lecture on "The Role of Private Members in Parliament!'. The lecture which was attended by an august gathering was presided over by Hon'ble Speaker Lok Sabha, Shri G.M.C. Balayogi.

Preparations for arranging other lecture are being made and the Institute is awaiting communications/ confirmations from dignitaries in this regard.

The Institute's proposal for organising the seminar on 'Population Issues' is still awaiting confirmation from the States. The Institute is making all preparations for organising the seminar but is awaiting communications from the States of Haryana, Gujarat, Uttar Pradesh and Madhya Pradesh whom the request has been made on instructions from the Union Ministry of Health and Family Welfare.

(v) Publications and Periodicals:

During the period under report the Institute brought out a publication on 'The Role of Governor and Article 356'. The Institute also continues to publish the English and Hindi Journals. The publication of Human Rights is in progress.

(vi) Library

A few books could be added to the library holdings due to shortage of funds but the library has, as usual, been receiving periodicals on complimentary/exchange basis as also literature from other organisations. The Institute has also been supplying its publications including the journals to States Assemblies, National libraries and other institutions on exchange/ complimentary basis all over the country and abroad. The library has been providing research and reference assistance to visiting scholars, and course participants, members of the Institute, as usual.

(vii) Forecast or the activities or the Institute for the period from 1st January to 31st March, 19":

The Institute would undertake the following activities during January-March, 1999:

To finalise the accounts and annual report and May, 1998 have these duly audited and passed by the Governing Body of the Institute.

Convene the meeting of the Executive Council as also the General Body of the institute to look after its different projects.

Follow up action on building Project work

Conduct different activities under the Parliamentary

Fellowship Programme and diploma courses e.g. (i) Organising some 30 lectures in the field of constitutional law and parliamentary institutions and processes, etc., for the benefit of members, course participants and staff members (ii) to arrange branch- in-training for the participants in the two secretariats of Parliament; (iii) to arrange visits and meetings of fellows around Delhi to meet dignitaries and senior officials as part of the programme.

To process the publication of G.V. Mavalankar Memorial Lecture organised in December, 1098.

To process other publications including two journals of the Institute.

To organise a memorial lecture/public lecture on topic in their field.

To take follow up action in the matter regrading organisation of seminars which are already under consideration of the Institute.

To make available research and reference service to members, course participants and staff and visiting scholars as a regular feature of the Institute's library. Books and periodicals would also be added to the library collections as usual.

International centre for alternative dispute resolutioin

The organizational set-up of the ICADR continued to be the same as was in the year 1997-98, namely:

The General Body,

The Governing Council,

The Chairperson,

The Secretary-General,

The Treasurer, and

The Secretary

The new Secretary-General joined the ICADR on 1st

The Governing Council of the ICADR held its meetings on 1st May, 1998 and 12th September, 1998. General Body meeting of the ICADR, was held on 12th September, 1998.

The following Training Programme and Seminars/ Workshops were organised by the ICADR during the period under consideration:

The thirteenth Seminar on "Maritime Arbitration" was organised by the ICADR on the 27th April, 1998 in its premises at New Delhi. The Seminar was inaugurated by Shri Deepak Das Gupta, Secretary to the Government of India, Ministry of Surface Transport. It was attended by 22 participants. The Seminar was organised to acquaint the participants with the new concepts of ADR and Conciliation in relation to maritime disputes.

The Fourteenth Training Programme on "Arbitration and Conciliation" was organised by ICADR on 28th and 29th May, 1998 at Noida, near Delhi, exclusively for the benefit of Senior Executives of the National Thermal Power Corporation.

The Fifteenth Workshop on "Arbitration and Conciliation" was organised on 17th and 18th July, 1998 at the ICADR's Regional Office at Hyderabad. The Workshop was inaugurated by the Chief Justice of Andhra Pradesh High Court, Mr. Justice U.C. Banerjee. It was attended by 31 participants. The participants represented Local Bar, Public Sector Undertakings and Private Industries, Certificates to the participants were distributed by the Chief Secretary to the Government of Andhra Pradesh, Mr. Madhav Rao, IAS.

The Sixteenth Training Programme on "Arbitration

and Construction Management" was organised by the ICADR in its premises at New, Delhi on 5th September, 1998. The programme was inaugurated by Mr. Justice K.N. Singh, former Chief Justice of India anti Chairman, Law Commission of India. It was attended by 28 participants. The Seminar was organised to inform the participants about ADR and Conciliation methods in relation to dispute arising out of the Contracts for Construction.

A "Conference on Dispute Resolution" took place at New Delhi on 12th and 13th December, 1998. The Conference on 12th December, 1998 was organised by the ICADR at the Hotel Intercontinental at New Delhi and was inaugurated by the Chief Justice of India. It was attended by the Judges of the Supreme Court and High Courts, Lawyers from Chandigarh, Haryana, Uttar Pradesh, Rajasthan and Madhya Pradesh. Senior Advocates like Shri K.K. Venugopal, Shri P.P. Rao, Dr. A.M. Singhvi, Shri R.N. Trivedi, Addl. Solicitor General for India expressed their views in the Conference. The Conference on 13th December, 1998 was organised in collaboration with the Institute of Company Secretaries of India and the Bar Council of India and was inauguarated by Mr. Justice A.M. Ahmadi, former Chief Justice of India. Mr. Justice D.P. Wadhwa, Judge, Supreme Court presided over the Conference Mr. F.S. Nariman, Senior Advocate also spoke on the occasion.

Rt. Hon'ble 'The Lord Cooke of Thorndon, KBE of the House of Lords, delivered the Special Address on both the days.

About five hundred persons-mainly from the profession of Law and Chartered Accountancy, Company Secretaries and heads of Public and Private Sector Organisations participated in the Conference.

Matters relating to the Construction of office complex

by the ICADR on the land allotted to it by the DDA at Vasant Kunj Phase II (Institutional Area) are being vigorously pursued. Three meetings of the Building Committee constituted by the Governing Council of the ICADR have already been held and selection of an architect for the project is nearly finalised. Government of India has been approached to release the grant for construction of the office complex.

Vigorous Drive has been undertaken to e new members of the ICADR and considerable sue is expected to be achieved very soon.

Efforts air being continued to contact the various State Governments to extend their cooperation for the establishment of ICADR's regional offices in their States.

Forecast of likely developments during the remaining period of the current financiall, year i.e. January to 31st March, 1999

A broad indication of the likely developments/activities of die ICADR from 1st January to 31st March, 1999 is given below:

A Seminar/Workshop on "ADR and related matters" is planned to be held in January, 1999 at the ICADR's Regional Central at Hyderabad.

A Seminar on 'ADR' is being organised in January, 1999 at Chennai in collaboration with Local Law Officers Association of Public Sector Undertakings.

A Seminar/Workshop is being planned at Chandigarh at the end of January, 1999 with the active participation of the local Bar.

A Training Programme in "ADR and Conciliation" is also planned at Lucknow in the month of February, 1999 with the active support of the Uttar Pradesh Government and the Bar.

A series of meeting have already been held and are

planned to popularise the ICADR and its activities, e.g., meeting of chiefs of Solicitors firms in and outside Delhi, a meeting of junior advocates working with Senior advocates of Supreme Court/High Court. A few meetings of Chief Executives/Law officers of Public and Private Sector Undertakings, etc., are also planned.

Managements of Public Sector Undertakings, such as ONGC, GAIL, LIC, GIC, Banks, Escorts, Voltas, Siemans and such other business giants will be approached to entrust the ICADR with the task of training their executives in the method of ADR and Conciliation, Mediation, etc. They are also being requested to incorporate in their agreements that their disputes with other parties be referred to ICADR.

The ICADR also proposes to start for the first time in India a regular Diploma Courses in Arbitration, Conciliation and other ADR methods at Delhi and Hyderabad. It is proposed to get the courses recognised by the Government of India or some University.

The ICADR also proposes to bring out a monthly "News Letter" to popularise the new concept of ADR and Conciliation in the country.

2

Legislative Department

The Legislative Department is concerned mainly with the following matters:

(i) Scrutiny of Notes for the Cabinet in relation to all legislative proposals from drafting and constitutional points of view;

(ii) Drafting of all Government Bills including Constitution (Amendment) Bills before introduction it) Parliament; translation of all such Bills into Hindi and forwarding of both English and Hindi versions of the Bills to the Parliament Secretariat; drafting of Government amendments to Bills, scrutiny of nonofficial amendments and rendering of assistance to Administrative Ministries to decide on the acceptability or otherwise of non-official amendments;

(iii) Rendering assistance to Parliament and Joint Select or Standing Committees of Parliament at all states through which a Bill passes before enactment. This includes scrutiny of and/or preparation of reports of such Committees, and Hindi translations of such reports anti minutes of dissent;

(iv) Drifting of Ordinance, to be promulgated by the President;

(v) Drafting of legislations to be enacted as President's Acts in respect of States under President's rule;

(vi) Drafting of Regulations to be made by the President;

(vii) Drafting of Constitution Orders, i.e. Orders required to be issued under the Constitution;

(viii) Scrutiny of all statutory rules, orders and notifications and their translation into Hindi;

(ix) Scrutiny of State Legislations in the Concurrent field which requires assent of the President under article 254 of the Constitution;

(x) Scrutiny of legislations to be enacted by Union territory Legislatures;

(xi) Election to Parliament, Legislatures of States and Union territories and Offices of the President and Vice-President;

(xii) Apportionment of expenditure on elections between the Centre and the States/Union territories with Legislatures;

(xiii) Election Commission, Electoral Reforms;

(xiv) Publication of Central Acts, Ordinances and Regulations, and their authorised translations in Hindi and other languages specified in the Eighth Schedule to the Constitution.

During the period 1998-99 (i.e. from 1st April, 1998 to 31st January, 1999) this Department examined under 131 Notes for the Cabinet involving legislative proposals in consultation with different Ministries/ Departments concerned for drafting Bills for introduction in the Houses of Parliament. Out of the Bills which were pending before Parliament and those introduced during the period, 34 Bills were enacted into Acts during the period. Some important Acts enacted during the period are surveyed below, in chronological order.

Important Enactments

The Income-tax (Amendment) Act, 1998 (7 of 1998): Generally, the basis on which depreciation is claimed by an assessee is the written down value of the block of assets. To enable power generating units to depreciate their capital assets in a straight line method at the same rate at which it is reimbursed by the State Electricity Boards under the Electricity (Supply) Act, 1948, section 32 of the Income-tax Act has been amended. In order to provide incentives to mineral oil, power, highway projects and undertakings located in industrially backward districts of the country, section 80-1A has been amended so as to:

(i) extend the benefit of deduction available to undertakings commencing production of mineral oil in the North-Eastern region to undertakings located in other parts of country commencing commercial production of mineral oil on or after 1st April, 1997;

(ii) extend the benefit of deduction available to infrastructure facility to housing and other development activities which are integral part of a highway project with a condition that the profits of such housing and other development activities shall be ploughed back to hi-Away projects within a period of three years;

(iii) extend time limit for availing the tax holiday from 12 years to 20 years in respect of highway and express-way projects;

(iv) extend the cut off date for availing the tax benefit by undertakings which generate or generate and distribute power from 31st March, 1998 to 31st March, 2000; and

(v) provide for a five year tax holiday to undertakings located in the notified industrially backward districts of category 'A' and a three year-tax holiday to undertakings located in the notified industrially backward districts of category 'B'; subject to the condition that such undertakings begin to manufacture or produce articles or things or to operate cold storage plant or plants at any time during the period from 1. 10. 1994 to 31.3.1999. In both the cases, the tax holiday period will be followed by the benefit of deduction of twenty-five per cent of profits (thirty per cent in case of companies) for five years to the eligible undertakings.

For the same purpose the Income-tax (Amendment) Ordinance, 1997 (Ordinance 15 of 1997) was promulgated on the 16th September, 1997 to achieve the above purposes. As the Income-tax (Amendment) Ordinance, 1997 could not be replaced by an Act of Parliament due to the dissolution of the House of die People, the President promulgated the Income-tax (Amendment) Second Ordinance, 1997 (Ord. 28 of 1997) on the 26th December, 1997. This Ordinance was replaced by the Income-tax (Amendment) Act, 1998 (7 of 1998).

The Merchant Shipping (Amendment) Act, 1998 (9 of 1998): One of the objectives of the Merchant Shipping Act, 1958 is to foster and ensure efficient maintenance of Indian Mercantile marine sector to best sub-serve the nation's interests. Indian merchant ships are required to comply with various International Conventions to which India is a party. ILO Convention No. 147 stipulates safety standards, including standards of competency, hours of work and manning so as to ensure safety of life on board ship, etc. Since India is a signatory to the said Convention, it became necessary to amend the Merchant Shipping Act, 1958 to the extent of dealing with the complaints from Indian seamen on foreign vessels and, foreign seamen on foreign vessels in the Indian territorial waters. The said ILO Convention came into force in India w.e.f. 26th September, 1997. As Parliament was not in session, the President promulgated the Merchant Shipping

(Amendment) Ordinance, 1997 (Ord. 19 of 1997) on the 26th September, 1997. As the Bill to replace the said Ordinance could not be introduced in die Rajya Sabha and Lok Sabha had been dissolved by the President on the 4th December, 1997 the President repromulgated the Merchant Shipping (Amendment) Second Ordinance, 1997 (Ord. 27 of 1997) on the 25th December, 1997 so as to have continuity of amendment made in the Merchant Shipping Act. After constitution of the 12th Lok Sabha the Parliament had a short Session in February, 1998 and in that session as the normal legislative business could not be taken up, it became essential to again repromulgate the Ordinance for the third time on 23rd April, 1998 i.e. the Merchant Shipping (Amendment) Ordinance, 1998 (Ord. 7 of 1998) so as to have continued effect of the above amendment.

The Merchant Shipping (Amendment) Act, 1998 has been passed by Parliament, which received the assent of the President on 22nd June, 1998, replacing the aforesaid Ordinance.

The Employees' Provident Funds and Miscellaneous Provisions (Amendment) Act, 1998 (10 of 1998): The Employees' Provident- Funds and Miscellaneous Provisions Act, 1952 provides for the institution of compulsory provident fund, pension fund and deposit-linked insurance for the benefit of employees in factories and establishments. While examining the Demands for Grants for the Ministry of Labour, the Standing Committee of Parliament on Labour and Welfare had made certain suggestions for amendment of the Act. The Employees' Provident Funds and Miscellaneous Provisions (Amendment) Bill, 1997 was introduced in Rajya Sabha, inter alia, to provide for the following:-

(i) to raise the minimum rate of provident fund contribution from 8.33 per cent to 10 per cent and the maximum rate from 10 per cent to 12 per cent of the monthly wages in order to promote saving and ensure availability of higher retiral benefits;

(ii) to make a provision that a person who is, or has been, or is qualified to be a Judge of a High Court or a District Judge shall be eligible for appointment as the Presiding Officer of the Appellate Tribunal;

(iii) to abolish the provision of three years' infancy period so as to bring the factories/ establishments within the scope of the Act from the date of their establishment/ registration.

The Bill was introduced but could not be passed by the Parliament as both Houses were not in session. To achieve the purposes of the aforesaid Bill, the employees' Provident Funds and Miscellaneous. Provisions (Amendment) Ordinance, 1997 (Ord. 17 of 1997) was promulgated by the President on the 22nd September, 1997. The Eleventh Lok Sabha was dissolved on the 4th December, 1997. Therefore, to give continued effect to the provisions of the said Ordinance, the Employees' Provident Funds and Miscellaneous Provisions (Amendment) Second Ordinance, 1997 (Ord. 25 of 1997) was promulgated by (be President on the 25th December, 1997. As the Bill to replace the aforesaid Ordinance could not be passed during the Twelfth Lok Sabha in February, 1998, the Ordinance was repromulgated for the third time on the 23rd April, 1998, as the Employees' Provident Funds and Miscellenous Provisions (Amendment) Ordinance, 1998 (Ord. 8 of 1998).

The Employees' Provident Funds and Miscellaneous Provisions (Amendment) Bill, 1998 has been passed by the Parliament and received the assent of the President on 23rd June, 1998 replacing the aforesaid Ordinance.

The Payment of Gratuity (Amendment) Act, 1998 (11 or

1998): The Payment of Gratuity Act, 1972 provides for payment of gratuity to employees engaged in factories, mines, oilfields, plantations, ports, railway companies, shops and other establishments. On receipt of representations from trade unions, the Payment of Gratuity (Amendment) Bill, 1997 was introduced in Parliament to enhance the amount of gratuity from rupees one lakh to rupees two lakhs and fifty thousand. As the Bill could not be passed, the President promulgated on the 24th September, 1997, the Payment of Gratuity (Amendment) Ordinance, 1997 (Ord. 18 of 1997) to give effect to the provisions of the said Bill. As the Eleventh Lok Sabha was dissolved, the President promulgated, on the 25th December, 1997, the Payment of Gratuity (Amendment) Second Ordinance, 1997 (Ord. 26 of 1997) to give continued effect to the provisions of the said Ordinance. As the Bill could not be passed by Parliament immediately after the constitution of the 12th Lok Sabha, the President repromulgated, on the 23rd April, 1999, the Payment of Gratuity (Amendment) Ordinance, 1998 (Ord. 10 of 1998) to give continued effect to the provisions of the earlier Ordinance.

The Payment of Gratuity (Amendment) Act, 1998 was passed by Parliament and assented to by the President on 22nd June, 1998. This Act enhances the amount of gratuity from rupees one lakh to rupees three lakhs and fifty thousand (instead of rupees two lakhs, and fifty thousand as provided in the Ordinance) keeping in view the Fifth Pay Commission's recommendations and consequent increase in the amount of gratuity payable to Government employees.

The Representation of People (Amendment) Act, 1998 (12 or 1998): Clause (6) of article 324 of the Constitution provides that, on the request of the Election Commission, the President or Governor of a State shall make available to the Election Commission such staff as may be necessary for the discharge of its functions. Further section 159 of the Representation of the People Act, 1951 provides that every local authority in a State shall, when so requested by a Regional Commissioner or the Chief Electoral Officer of the State, make available to any returning officer such staff as may be necessary for the performance of any duties in connection with an election.

The Supreme Court, in its judgement in Civil Appeal No. 6026 of 1993 Election Commission of India vs. State Bank of India Staff Association, Patna and others and Civil Appeal No. 4611 of 1989 Election Commission of India Vs. Northern Zone Insurance Employees Association, Rajasthan (AIR 1995 SC 1078) held that the Election Commission cannot requisition the services of employees of State Bank of India and the Life Insurance Corporation of India for election duties as such employees are neither employees of the Central Government nor of a State Government nor of a local authority and observed that the persons whose services may be placed at the disposal of the Election Commission must be either employees of the Central Government or of the State Government or of a local authority. In view of the aforesaid judgment, and to make available the staff of statutory and non-statutory bodies aided by the Government, or universities and other educational institutions aided by the Government, and because of the impending General Elections to the 12th Lok Sabha, the President promulgated the Representation of the People (Amendment) Ordinance, 1997 (Ord. 23 of 1997) on the 23rd December, 1997 which provides for requisitioning of services for election work of employees of, apart from local authorities, every university and any other institution, concern or undertaking (not being an institution, concern or undertaking established under a Central, Provincial or State Act or a company within the meaning of section 617 of the Companies Act, 1956) controlled, or financed wholly or substantially by funds provided, directly or indirectly, by the Central Government or a State Government. The President promulgated the Representation of the People (Amendment) Ordinance, 1998 (Ord. 12 of 1998) on the 24th April, 1998 to give continued effect to the provisions of the aforesaid 1997-Ordinance and to avoid any difficulty to the Election Commission in holding elections in the interregnum.

The Representation of the People (Amendment) Act, 1998 has been passed to replace the aforesaid Ordinance of 1998. This Amendment Act also has brought under the ambit of section 159 of the Representation of the People Act, employees of public sector enterprises, etc.

The National Institute of Pharmaceutical Education and Research Act, 1998 (13 of 1998): The National Institute of Pharmaceutical Education and Research set up as an autonomous body in 1991, was registered as a society under the Societies Registration Act, 1860. A Bill to declare the National Institute of Pharmaceutical Education and Research to be an Institution of national importance under Entry 64 of List I of the Seventh Schedule to the Constitution and to provide for its incorporation and matters connected therewith was introduced in the Lok Sabha on 3rd March, 1997. The Bill lapsed on the dissolution of the Eleventh Lok Sabha. In order to ensure that the process of enrolment of students is not delayed, the National Institute of Pharmaceutical Education and Research Ordinance, 1998 (Ord. 2 of 1998) was promulgated on 21st January, 1998 for the purpose. Since the Ordinance was to lapse on the expiry of six weeks after the reassembly of Parliament, that is, on 5th May, 1998, the National Institute of Pharmaceutical Education and Research (Second) Ordinance, 1998 (Ord. 9 of 1998) was promulgated on 23rd April, 1998 to give continued effect to the provisions of the aforesaid Ordinance.

To replace the aforesaid Ordinance the National Institute of Pharmaceutical Education and Research Bill, 1998 was passed by Parliament which received the assent of the President on 26th June, 1998.

The Electricity Regulatory Commissions Act, 1998 (14 of 1998): Power sector in India is beset with problems that impede its capacity to respond to the rapidly growing demand for energy. Although the initial measures had been taken, serious problems persist, and the reform becomes increasingly difficult underscoring the need to act decisively and without delay, to focus on fundamental issues facing the power sector, namely, lack of rational retail tariffs, high level of cross-subsidies, poor planning and operation, inadequate capacity, neglect of consumers, limited involvement of private sector skills and resources and the absence of an independent regulatory authority. Considering the paramount importance of re-structuring the power sector, two conferences of Chief Ministers were organised to discuss the whole gamut of issues in the power sector. A Common Minimum Plan for Power (CMNEP) was adopted at these conferences. The CMNEP recognised that the gap between demand and supply of power is widening and acknowledged that the financial position of State Electricity Boards is fast deteriorating and future development in the power sector cannot be sustained without viable State Electricity Boards and improvement of their operational performance. The CMNEP identified creation of Regulatory Commission as a step in this direction and specifically provides for establishment of Central Electricity Regulatory Commission (CPRC) and State Electricity Regulatory Commissions (SERCs). The Administrative Staff College of India, Hyderabad was assigned the task of studying the restructuring needs of the regulatory system and the report of the ASCI recommended the creation of independent Electricity Regulatory Commissions, both at the Centre and the States.

To give effect to the above proposals, the Electricity Regulatory Commission Bill, 1997 was introduced in Lok Sabha on 14th August, 1997. This Bill could not be passed due to dissolution of the Eleventh Lok Sabha, which resulted in delay in establishing the Regulatory Commission leading to confusion and misgivings in various sections about Government's commitment to the reforms and restructuring or the power sector. Therefore, it was considered necessary to ensure the speedy establishment of the Regulatory Commissions and as Parliament was not in session, the President promulgated the Electricity Regulatory Commissions Ordinance, 1998 (Ord. 14 of 1998) on 25th day of April, 1998.

The salient features of the said Ordinance were as follows:

(a) it provides for the establishment of a Central Electricity Regulatory Commission at the Central level and State Electricity Commissions at the State levels.

(b) the main functions of CERC are:-

  (i) to regulate the tariff of generating companies owned or controlled by the Central Government;

  (ii) to regulate inter-State transmission including tariff of the transmission utilities;

  (iii) to regulate inter-State sale of power;

  (iv) to aid and advise die Central Government in the formulation of tariff policy:

(c) the main functions of the SERC, to start with shall be:

  (i) to determine the tariff for electricity, wholesale, bulk, grid and retail;

  (ii) to determine the tariff payable for use of the transmission facilities;

(iii) to regulate power purchase and procurement process of the transmission utilities, etc.

(iv) subsequently, as and when each State Government notifies, other regulatory functions could also be assigned to SERCs;

(d) it also aims at improving the financial health of the State Electricity Boards (SEBs) which are losing heavily on account of irrational tariffs and Lack of budgetary support from the State Governments, as a result of which, the SEBs have become incapable of even proper maintenance, leave alone purposive investment. Further, the lack of creditworthiness of SEBs has been a deterrent in attracting investment both from the public and private sectors. Hence, it is made mandatory for State Commissions to fix tariff in a manner that none of the consumers or class of consumers shall be charged less than fifty per cent of the average cost of supply. It enables the State Governments to exercise the option of providing subsidies to weaker sections on condition that the State Governments through a subsidy, compensate the SEBs. As regards the agricultural sector, it provides that if the State Commission considers it necessary, it may allow the consumers in the agricultural sector to be charged less than fifty per cent for a maximum period of three years from the date of commencement of the Ordinance. It also empowers the State Government to reduce the tariff further but in that case it shall compensate die SEBs or its successor utility, the difference between the tariff fixed by the State Commission and the tariff proposed by the State Governments by providing budgetary allocations. Therefore, it enables the State Governments to fix any tariff for agriculture and other sectors provided it gives subsidy to State Electricity Boards to meet the loss.

To replace the aforesaid Ordinance the Electricity Regulatory Commission Act, 1998 was passed by the Parliament, which received the assent of the President on the 2nd July, 1998.

The Finance (Amendment) Act, 1998 (16 of 1998): Consequent upon the finalisation of the decision on the Fifth Pay Commission's recommendations, a review of the expenditure budget for 1997-98 was undertaken. The review revealed that post budget commitments as well as the Pay Commission's award added up to a total expenditure beyond the budget estimates. A number of proposals for additional expenditure were also pending consideration. These developments indicated a slippage in the fiscal deficit, which could send negative signals to the financial market, impact on interest and inflow of investment. To mop up additional resources, raising of special duty of customs leviable under section 68 of the Finance (No. 2) Act, 1996 from 2 per cent to 5 per cent. ad valorem on imported goods (other than petroleum products and project imports), and raising of foreign travel tax leviable under section 35 of the Finance Act, 1979 in respect of journeys undertaken to non-neighbouring countries from Rs. 300 to Rs.750 per passenger were decided. Since the Parliament was not in session, the Finance Acts (Amendment) Ordinance, 1997 (Ord. 16 of 1997) was promulgated on the 16th September, 1997 for the purpose.

The said Ordinance could not be replaced by a Bill in the Winter Session of Parliament in 1997. To give continued effect to the provisions of the said Ordinance, the Finance (Second Amendment) Ordinance, 1997 (Ord. 24 of 1997) was promulgated on 24th December, 1997 with the modification that the foreign travel tax for journeys undertaken to non-neighbouring countries be charged at the rate of Rs. 500 per passenger in place of Rs.750 per passenger with effect from 1st January, 1998.

The said Ordinance also could not be replaced by a Bill during the fast session of the Twelfth Lok Sabha. Therefore, further to give continued effect to the said proposals, the Finance (Amendment) Ordinance, 1998 (Ord. 5 of 1998) was promulgated by the President on 21st April, 1998. To replace the aforesaid Ordinance, Parliament passed the Finance (Amendment) Bill, !998, which received the assent of the President on 7th July, 1998.

The Lotteries (Regulation) Act, 1998 (17 of 1998): The conduct of certain types of lottery in the country, the malpractices thereof and their impact on poorer sections of the society had been under scrutiny of the Government. The continued prevalence of, popularly known, single digit and instant lotteries and the temptation offered by them proved to be the undoing of many families. In spite of the guidelines issued by the Central Government as also the guidelines issued by the Hon'ble Supreme Court, the evil could not be eliminated and a need to regulate the conduct of lotteries through the Central Legislation became necessary to protect the interests of the gullible poor. Considering the exigencies of the matter and as the Parliament was not in session, the Lotteries (Regulation) Ordinance, 1997 (Ord. 20 of 1997) was promulgated by the President on 1st October, 1997. In order to give continued, effect to the provisions of the said Ordinance, the Lotteries (Regulation) Second Ordinance, 1997 (Ord. 31 of 1997) was promulgated by the President on 30th December, 1997. As the Lotteries (Regulation) Second Ordinance, 1997 (Ord. 31 of 1997) was going to lapse on the 5th May, 1998, the President promulgated, on 23rd April, 1998 the Lotteries (Regulation) Ordinance, 1998 (Ord. 6 of 1998).

The Lotteries (Regulation) Act, 1998 replacing the aforesaid Ordinance was passed by the Parliament. The Act provides, inter alia, for conditions subject to which lotteries may be organised, such as prizes not to be offered on pre-announced number or on the basis of a single digit,

State Governments to print lottery tickets bearing the imprint and logo of the State, the State Government to sell the tickets either itself or through the distributors or selling agents, the State Governments to conduct the draws of all the lotteries, place of draw to be located within the State,, lotteries not have more than one draw in a week, number of bumper draws not to be more than six in a calendar year, etc. The Act also provides that the State Government may, within the State, prohibit the sale of lottery tickets of another State and the Central Government may prohibit the lottery organised in contravention of the conditions, etc. The offences under the Act have been made cognizable and non bailable.

The High Court and Supreme Court Judges (Conditions of Service) Amendment Act, 1998 (18 of 1998): The Fifth Central Pay Commission recommended the revision in the salaries and other allowances of the Central Government employees including the members of All India Services. The Government has accepted the majority of the recommendations. The notification dated the 30th September, 1997 amending the pay rules of the Central Government employees namely, the Central Civil Service (Revised Pay) Rules, 1997, has also been issued. The revised pay rules are deemed to have come into force on the 1st day of January, 1996.

Having considered all aspects of the matter, a necessity was fell to increase the salaries of the Judges with effect from the 1st January, 1996 as detailed below:-

Chief Justice of India	Rs. 33,000 per month
Judges of the Supreme Court	Rs. 30,000 per month
Chief Justice of a High Court	Rs. 30,000 per month
Judges of High Court	Rs. 26,000 per month.

Since the Parliament was not in session, the President promulgated the High Court and Supreme Court Judges (Conditions of Service) Amendment Ordinance, 1998 (Ord.

II of 1998) on the 24th day of April, 1998 to give effect to the increase in the salaries of the Judges.

The High Court and the Supreme Court Judges (Conditions of Service) Amendment Act, 1998 replaced die said Ordinance.

The Electricity Laws (Amendment) Act, 1998 (22 of 1998): Ibis Act provides for transmission as a distinct activity independent of generation and distribution under the Indian Electricity Act, 1910 and the Electricity (Supply) Act, 1948 and to empower the Central Government or the Central Electricity Regulatory Commission to grant transmission license in the case of inter-State transmission of energy and the State Government or the State Electricity Regulatory Commission in the case of intra-State transmission of energy in the area of transmission to he specified in the license.

The Interest on Delayed Payments to Small Scale and Ancillary Industrial Undertakings (Amendment) Act, 1998 (23 of 1998): The Interest on Delayed Payments to Small Scale and Ancillary Industrial Undertakings Act, 1993 regulates the procedure for payment of interest on delayed payments to small scale and ancillary undertakings. Though the Act has been in operation for a period of five years, the problem of delays in payment of outstanding dues to the small scale industrial units continues unabated. There have been widespread discussions on the provisions of the Act among the various interest groups including the Departments of State Governments dealing with industries, banks and Small Industry Associations'. The general consensus emerged from such discussions is that certain amendments to the Act are necessary in order to make it more effective so that the aims and objectives of the Act are achieved.

The existing Act is not applicable to the Central or

State public sector undertakings, such as, the National Small Industries Corporation (NSIC) and the State Small Industries Development Corporations (SSIDC). Since both the aforesaid Corporations have been playing important role in marketing of SSI products, this Act amends the definition of "supplier" so as to bring within the scope; the aforesaid Corporations.

Section 3 of the Act stipulates that a buyer is required to make payment on or before the agreed date to small scale supplier of goods or services. Where the credit period is not specified in the agreement, the payment is to be made within 30 days from the date of the acceptance of goods or services. It has been noticed that buyers tend to prescribe a credit period of 240—360 days. This defeats the purpose of the Act. 11 also amends section 3 of the Act by specifying a period of 120 days as the maximum period of credit.

Section 4 of the Act states that buyers shall be liable to pay interest to the suppliers on outstanding dues; beyond the appointed day at 4 rate which is five per cent points above the floor rate. The Reserve Bank of India, in its new credit policy, has changed the system of prescribing floor rates for the purpose of lending by hanks for the loans exceeding Rs. 2 lakhs. The banks are now free to fix the prime lending rate for loans. The change in interest rate policy has necessitated a change in determining the penal rate of interest in the Act. This Act has also fixed the penal rate of interest at one and a half times of the prime lending rate of the State Bank of India.

Under section 6 of the Act, the outstanding amount together with the interest is recoverable (in case of dispute) by way of' a civil suit. This Act also further provides an alternative mechanism of arbitration and conciliation apart from section 6 to resolve the disputes under the Act. For this purpose, State Governments have been authorised to set up one or more "Industry Facilitation Councils". For the purpose of arbitration and conciliation. These Councils shall act as arbitrators or conciliation for sectt. disputes between SSI suppliers and buyers. This aims of facilitating resolution of disputes between the two parties amicably.

The Beedi Workers Welfare Cess (Amendment) Act, 1998 (24 of 1998): The Beedi Workers Welfare Cess Act, 1976 (56 of 1976) and the Beedi Workers Welfare Funds Act, 1976 (62 of 1976) have been enacted to ameliorate the living conditions and provide welfare measures to beedi workers. The former Act provides for levy as a duty of excise by way of cess on manufactures beedis at a rate of not less than ten paise or mote than fifty paise per thousand. The proceeds are being utilised to finance the Welfare Fund for Beedi Workers. Initially, the case was fixed at twenty-rive paise per kilogram of tobacco issued from warehouses for manufacture of beedis. The cess for financing the Beedi Workers Welfare Fund could not be collected under the Beedi Workers, Welfare Cess Act, 1976 with effect from 1st the March, 1979 due to exemption granted by the Finance Act, 1979-80. Thereafter, the Beedi Workers Welfare Cess Act, 1976 was amended in 1981 to provide levy of not less than ten paise and not mote than fifty paise per thousand manufactured beedis.

After amendment of the Beedi Workers Welfare Cess Act, 1976, the cess was levied at the rate of ten paise per thousand manufacture beedis, but was increased to thirty paise pet thousand on 1st March, 1987 to meet the increasing cost of administering the various welfare measures under the Fund. It was subsequently increased to fifty paise per thousand manufacture beedis with effect from 17th October, 1995. In order to continue and expand welfare measures for persons employed in beedi establishments, the Beedi Workers Welfare Cess Act, 1976 has further been amended so as to increase the minimum rate of cess from ten paise to fifty paise and maximum rate of cess from fifty paise to five rupees per thousand manufacture beedis, as the Central Government may, from time to time, fix.

The President's Emoluments and Pension (Amendment) Act, 1998 (25 of 1998): Section IA of the President's Emoluments and Pension Act, 1951 provides that there shall be paid to President by way of emoluments twenty thousand rupees per mensem. Subsection (1) of section 2 of the Act provides for pension of one lakh twenty thousand rupees per annum to the retiring Presidents.

The emoluments and pension of President were last enhanced in 1990. Consequent upon the revision of the salary and allowances of various constitutional functionaries, it is considered necessary to enhance the emoluments of President and pension to the retiring Presidents. In view of this the emoluments of President has been enhanced from rupees twenty thousand per mensem to rupees fifty thousand per mensem and pension from rupees one lakh twenty thousand per annum to rupees three lakhs per annum.

As the Vice-President's Pension Act, 1997 has been enacted to provide for payment of pension and other pensionary benefits to such persons who have held the office of the Vice-President of India, it is considered that the pension and the other facilities admissible to such persons who have held the office of the Vice President of India and subsequently becomes entitled to pension under the President's Emoluments and Pension Act, 1951 may not be extended. Therefore, such a restriction under the President's Emoluments and Pension Act, 1951 has also been imposed.

The Salaries and Allowances of Officers of Parliament (Amendment) Act, 1998 (26 of 1998): Consequent upon the enhancement in the President's emoluments and Pension

Act, 1951, and in the Salary, Allowances and pension of members of Parliament the total emoluments of the Chairman of the Council of States have also been raised to Rs. 40,000/- per month with effect from the 1st January, 1996 which is considered to be a reasonable level between the emoluments payable to the President of India and those likely to be payable to the Governor of a State.

The Governors (Emoluments, Allowances and Privileges) Amendment Act, 1998 (27 of 1998): Clause (3) of article 158 of the Constitution provides that the Governors shall be entitled to such emoluments, allowances and privileges, as may be determined by Parliament by law, and until a provision in that behalf is so made, they will receive such emoluments, allowances and privileges as are specified under the Second Schedule to the Constitution. Parliament has enacted the Governors (Emoluments, Allowances and Privileges) Act, 1982 to provide for the emoluments, allowances and other privileges to Governors and section 3 thereof prescribes rupees eleven thousand per mensem as emoluments thereof. The above emoluments were made effective from 1st April, 1986.

Consequent upon the revision of salary and allowances of various constitutional authorities, it was considered necessary to enhance the emoluments of the Governors of States. There has been considerable price-rise since 1996 and the emoluments and allowances of the Governors have not been enhanced since then. It was, therefore, felt appropriate to enhance their emoluments which were last revised in 1986 and thus the emoluments of the Governors was raised from rupees eleven thousand per-mensem to rupees thirty-six thousand per mensem with effect from 1st January, 1996

The Salary, Allowances and Pension of Me in, hers of Parliament (Amendment) Act, 1998 (28 of 1998): The Joint Parliamentary Committee and the Joint Committee on

Salaries and Allowances of Members of Parliament have made several recommendations for increasing the salary, allowances and other facilities to Members of Parliament and pension to the former Members of Parliament. On the basis of the recommendations, it was proposed, inter alia, to increase the salary of Members of Parliament from rupees one thousand rive hundred to rupees four thousand per month, to raise the daily allowance from rupees two hundred to rupees four hundred, to increase the number of single air journeys from twenty-eight to thirty-two in a year with a provision that unutilized air journey of the year will be carried over to the following year, to increase in road mileage from rupees five to rupees six per kilometre, allowing road mileage to a Member of Parliament if he travels by road between the place connected by rail, to increase the minimum pension from rupees one thousand four hundred to rupees two thousand five hundred per month, to increase the additional pension from rupees two hundred and fifty to rupees five hundred for each year exceeding five years of service as such member, to increase in pension to the spouse or dependant of a Member of Parliament from rupees five hundred per month to rupees one thousand per month in case such member dies in harness. It was also proposed to increase the amount of car advance to a Member of Parliament from rupees fifty thousand to rupees one lakh and allow the spouse of the member to travel free in all rail journeys in air-conditioned first class or executive class in all trains from usual place of residence to Delhi and back against present to and fro air-conditioned two tier rail travel facilities once during each session.

Oilfields (Regulation and Development Amendment) Act, 1948 (29 of 1998): Sub-section (4) of section 6A of the Oilfields Regulation and Development) Act, 1948 empowers the Central Government to amend the Schedule to the said Act, by notification, so as to enhance or reduce the rate at which royalty shall be payable in respect of any mineral oil, subject to the condition that the rate of royalty in respect of any mineral oil shall not be fixed so as to exceed twenty per cent of the sale price of the mineral oil and that the rate of royalty in respect of any mineral oil shall not be enhanced more than once during any period of three years.

With a view to encourage exploration of oil and natural gas in the country, the Government approved the New Exploration Licensing Policy (NELP) providing, inter alia, for the following:-

(i) royalty rates for crude oil shall be at the rate of 12.5% for the onland areas and 10% for offshore areas, calculated with reference to international process;

(ii) royalty may be reduced or exempted with a view to encourage exploration in deep water areas and frontier areas. To begin with, royalty will be charged at half the prevailing rate for offshore areas beyond 400 metre bathymetry for the first seven years after the commencement of commercial production.

Thus, for the acreages to be offered under the NELP, royalty would be payable at different rates depending on the location of the area, water depth, etc. The present scheme of the Oilfields (Regulation and Development) Act, 1948, however, does not permit laying down of more than one rate of royalty in respect of any mineral oil, as required to operationalise the NELP. It was, therefore, necessary to amend the Oilfields (Regulation and Development) Act, 1948 for incorporating suitable provisions in section 6A of the said Act for conferring upon the Central Government the powers to notify the rates of royalty approved under the New Exploration Licensing Policy.

The Government also decided to dismantle the Administered pricing Mechanism (APM) in respect of it digenous crude oil and petroleum products in a released manner commencing from the 1st April, 1998. With this, the price of indigenous crude oil which was earlier fixed on a cost plus formula once in three years his been linked to the international FOB price of crudes imported into the country. Under the new pricing scheme, the price of indigenous crude oil would now vary on monthly basis. This necessitated some changes in the Act to make it possible to vary the rate of royalty on crude oil at intervals shorter than three year, as presently provided for in the Act.

To meet the above requirements, it was proposed to amend section 6A of the Act so as to:

(i) confer upon the Central Government the powers to notify more than one rate of royalty in respect of the same mineral oil produced from different classes of leased areas;

(ii) empower the Central Government to grant partial or full exemption from the payment of royalty in respect of offshore areas, and

(iii) make consequential amendments in section 10 of the Act for laying the notifications before Parliament.

The Act seeks to achieve the above objects.

The Export-Import Bank of India (Amendment) Act, 1998 (1 of 1999): Sub-section (1) of section 4 of the Export-Import Bank of India Act,. 1981 provides that the authorised capital of the Exim Bank shall be two hundred crores of rupees and the Central Government may, by notification, increase the said capital up to five hundred crores of rupees. The paid-up capital of the Exim Bank has been augmented every year out of the budgetary allocation and in the year 1995-96, it reached the maximum limit of five hundred crores of rupees.

It became necessary to provide for an adequate capital base to the Exim Bank to support its future business growth, to maintain its credit worthiness with international lenders, to enable it to raise external commercial borrowings at competitive rates for financing needs of Indian exporters, and to retain adequate resource flows for maintaining flexibility. Accordingly, it was proposed to raise the authorised capital of the Exim Bank from five hundred crores of rupees to one thousand from of rupees and enhance the maximum limit up to which the Central Government may increase the said capital, by notification in the official Gazette, from five hundred crores of rupees to two thousand crores of rupees. It was, therefore, necessary to amend sub-section (1) of section 4 of the Export-Import Bank of India Act.

The Cotton Ginning and Pressing Factories (Repeal) Act, 1998 (2 of 1999): The Cotton Ginning and Pressing Factories Act, 1925, enacted on the 8th day of August, 1925, provides for periodical filing of returns; maintenance of registers; marking of bales and other rule making powers for both the Central and State Governments for the purpose of regulating the ginning and pressing factories.

There have been changes in die pattern of processing, marketing and consumption of cotton since the enactment of the Act. In the market driven economy needing quality products modernisation of ginning and pressing factories is essential. In the present liberalized industrial scenario the restrictions laid down in the Cotton Ginning and Pressing Factories Act, 1925 are not required any longer and the Cotton Control Order, 1986 issued under the Essential Commodites Act, 1955 would cover provisions considered essential to regulate working of ginning and pressing factories in future so long as cotton remains as an essential commodity. Hence it was considered that the said Act should be repealed.

The repeal will also provide a thrust and incentive to the modernisation efforts in die cotton ginning and pressing sector to ensure quality processing of cotton and charging remunerative price for the service provided for.

This Act has been enacted to achieve the aforesaid objects.

The High Denomination Bank Notes (Demonetisation) Amendment Act, 1998 (3 of 1999): To eliminate the shortage of currency notes and to ease the pressure on other denominations, it was proposed to amend section 2 of the High Denomination Bank Notes (Demonetisation) Act, 1978. This will facilitate the Reserve Bank of India to issue notes of Rs. 1,000 denomination immediately.

The Railway Claims Tribunal (Amendment) Act, 1998 (4 of 1999): Section 9 of the Railway Claims Tribunal Act, 1987 provides that the salaries and allowances payable to, and the other terms and conditions of service (including pension, gratuity and other retirement benefits) of, the Chairman, vice Chairman and other Members shall be prescribed by rules. Accordingly, the Central Government notified the Railway Claims Tribunal (Salaries and Allowances and Conditions of Service of Chairman, Vice-Chairman and Members) Rules, 1989. While examining the question of revising the salary and allowances payable to the Chairman, Vice-Chairman and other Members of the Railway Claims Tribunal with effect from 1.1.1996 on the basis of the recommendations of the Fifth Central pay Commission by suitably amending the relevant rules, it was observed that there is no enabling provision in the said Act to give retrospective operation as provided under section 36A of the Administrative Tribunal Act, 1985. In order to overcome this difficulty, the said Act was amended to provide for an enabling provision to make rules with retrospective effect not earlier than the date of commencement of die said Act.

The Leaders and Chief Whips of Recognised Parties and Groups in Parliament (Facilities) Act, 1998 (5 or 1999): The Eleventh, All-India Whips' Conference held at Bangalore in January,' 1994 made the following recommendations:

Chief Whips of recognised Opposition Parties in Parliament and the State Legislatures should be provided secretarial assistance and facilities of telephone and office accommodation in the premises of Legislatures by giving them statutory recognition (Secretarial assistance means one Stenographer Grade 'B' and one Peon).

The Twelfth All India Whips' Conference held at Srinagar on 21st and 22nd August, 1997 further deliberated the issue relating to the facilities to be extended to Whips.

The smooth functioning of the parliamentary system depends to a large extent, on the efficiency of the party machinery in the legislatures. The Chief Whips and leader-, of parties and groups in Parliament are importing party functionaries who play a vital role in the proper functioning of' the parties and groups in the legislatures and hence fulfil an important public purpose.

After due consideration of the matter as a whole and to implement the recommendation of the All-India Whips' Conferences, this Act has been enacted provide for secretarial and telephone facilities to the Leaders and Chief Whips of recognised parties and recognised groups in Parliament.

The High Court and Supreme Court Judges (Salaries and Conditions of Service Amendment Act, 1998 (7 of 1999): When an officer of the State Judicial Service is appointed as a Judge of a High Court, his leave account is regulated under the provision of sub-clause (iii) of clause (a) of subsection (2) of section 4 of the High Court Judges (Salaries and Conditions of Service) Act, 1954, (hereinafter referred to as the 'High Court Judges; Act').

Under the aforesaid provision, a Judge is entitled to carry forward only the leave earned to the extent of two hundred and forty days. He is, however, not entitled to carry forward the half-pay leave in his leave account in the Judicial Service. Representations have been received from certain Judges, requesting for a provision in the High Court Judges Act to enable them to avail the benefit of carry-forward of half-pay leave. In view thereof, it was proposed to make a suitable amendment to the High Court Judges Act to provide for the same. Similarly, the Registry of the Supreme Court has requested for deleting the restrictions of two hundred and forty days for the carry-forward of leave on full allowances when a Judge of High Court is elevated to the Supreme Court. It was also proposed to accede to the request and the restriction of two hundred and forty days provided under section 4(2)(a)(iii) of the Supreme Court Judges (Salaries and Conditions of Service) Act, 1958, (hereinafter referred to as 'Supreme Court Judges Act') be done away with.

A High Court Judge or a Supreme Court Judge is entitled, without payment of rent, to the use of official residence. Where a Judge does not avail himself of the use of such residence he is paid every month an allowance, i.e. Rs. 2,500 per month in the case of a Judge of a High Court and Rs. 3,000 per month in the case of a Judge of the Supreme Court. Although there has been steep increase in the market rent of houses, die allowances payable to the Judges in lieu of official residence, has remained static since 1986. This acts as a serious disincentive for Judges to occupy their own houses and accept the facility of House Rent Allowance (HRA). Accordingly, it was further proposed to increase HRA to Rs. 10,000 per month in respect of the High Court and Supreme Court Judges.

The rates of pension of the Judges of the High Courts and the Supreme Court were last enhanced with effect from the 1st November, 1986 by the High Court and

Supreme Court Judges (Conditions of Service) Amendment Act, 1986. The Fifth Central Pay Commission recommended revision in the pensionary benefits of the Central Government employees including the members of Aft-India. Services. The revised pension rules have come into force on the 1st day of January, 1996. In view of foregoing, a necessity was felt to increase die pension, additional pension and maximum pension of the Judges of the High Courts and the Supreme Court suitably.

It was also proposed to enhance the entitlement of family pension from fifty per cent to sixty per cent of the pension admissible to a Judge up to the age of sixty-five years of such Judge had he survived or first seven years after his death, whichever is earlier, and thereafter from twenty-five per cent to thirty per cent of his pension subject to a minimum of Rs. 1,275 per month.

In the case of a Judge who has been elevated from the Bar, the existing provision provides for computation of death-cum-retirement gratuity amounting to 20 days' salary for each completed year of service unlike on half-yearly basis applicable to in the case of a Central Government employee. It was proposed to grant ten days' salary as gratuity for each completed one-half year of service.

It was also decided to remove the ceiling of Rs. 8 000 per annum as special additional pension in compliance with the order dated the 20th January, 1991 of the Supreme Court of India in the matter of Justice M. L. Jain Vs. Union of India.

This Act, therefore, amended the High Court Judges (Salaries and Conditions of Service) Act, 1954, and the Supreme Court Judges (Salaries and Conditions of Service) Act, 1958 to achieve the above objectives.

The Customs (Amendment) Act, 1998 (8 of 1999): Section

75A of the Customs Act, 1962, which was inserted by the Finance Act, 1995, provides that where any drawback payable to a claimant under section 74 or section 75 of the Customs Act as the case may be, is not paid within a period of three months from the date of riling of claim to the date of payment of such drawback, there shall be paid to the claimant in addition to the amount of drawback interest fixed under section 27A of the said Act from the date after the expiry of the said period of three months till the date of payment of such drawback.

With a view to arrest the declining trend in exports, several measures were announced by the Government in the recent past to give a special package of measures for boosting exports. One of the measures includes a commitment on the part of the Government, to pay interest to exporters if Government dues by way of duty drawback is delayed beyond two months. Thus, with a view to reduce the time-limit from three months to two months as given under section 75A of die Act, it was necessary to amend that section. The reduced time-limit of two months instead of the present three months will expedite the process of payment of drawback, and, thereby emphasise the urgency of delivering export related benefits to the exporters within shortest possible time.

Simultaneously, it was proposed to empower the Central Government to levy interest where the claimant has been sanctioned drawback erroneously, if such drawback is not refunded by him within a period of two months, instead of the present three months.

The amendments will expedite the process of payment of drawback and realization of revenue.

This Act seeks to achieve the above objects.

The Income-tax (Second Amendment) Act, 1998 (11 of 1999): This Act amends the Income-tax Act, 1961. The amendments made in the said Act are intended to extend and clarify certain fiscal incentives and to remove some anomalies in certain sections of the Income-tax Act.

Section 2 amends clause (23G) of section 10 of the Income-tax Act. This clause was amended by the Finance (No.2) Act, 1998 to provide, inter alia, &it the exemption under this clause shall be available in respect of the investments made on or after the 1st day of June, 1998 only in an enterprise which is wholly engaged in the business of developing, maintaining and operating an infrastructure facility and which has been approved by the Central Government. However, the amended provision generated apprehension among die tax payers that the benefit would not be available to investments made prior to 1.6-1998. The amendment seeks to clarify that the exemption available under said clause (23G) of Section 10 in respect of income from investment made before the 1st day of June, 1998 shall continue to be governed by the provisions of the said clause as it stood immediately before its amendment by the Finance (No.2) Act, 1998.

Section 3 amends section 10A of the Income-tax Act. Under the existing provisions, tax holiday is available, to newly established industrial undertakings set up in free trade zones and, to units set up in software technology parks for five years out of the block of initial eight years, subject to fulfilment of certain conditions. This amendment extends the period of tax holiday from five years to ten years in order to give added thrust to exports. Section 4 similarly extends the five year tax holiday period to ten years to the export-oriented units under section 10B of the Income-tax Act.

Section 5 amends section 32 of the Income-tax Act. With a view to remove sluggishness in commercial vehicles sector, the proposed amendment seeks to provide that depreciation on commercial vehicles acquired by the assessee on or after the 1st day of October, 1998 but before the 1st day of April 1999 and put to use before the 1st day of April, 1999 for the purposes of business, shall be allowed at full percentage prescribed for such assets, irrespective of the period of user of the assets during the relevant year.

Sections 6 and 7 amend sections 44AD and 44AE of the Income-tax Act respectively. These sections provide a presumptive basis to bring to tax the profits and gains arising from certain business. These sections allowed option to the assessees to declare a lower profit to tax than the profits determined on presumptive basis, subject to the condition that evidence in support of the profits so declared was furnished by the assessee and thereupon the assessment would be completed by scrutiny tinder section 143(3) of the Act. This option to declare the lower profit was withdrawn by the Finance Act, 1997 with effect from 1.4.1997. With a view to harmonize these provisions with sections 44AA and 44AB which provide for compulsory maintenance and audit thereof in such cases with effect from 1.4.1998, these amendments extend the benefit of option for offering lower profit under these sections for the assessment year 1997-98.

Section 8 amends section 80P of the Income-tax Act. Under the existing provision, profits derived by a co-operative society engaged in the marketing of agricultural produce of its members are fully deductible in computing the taxable income under section 80P(2)(a)(iii) of the Income-tax Act. The deduction was intended for primary, co-operative societies marketing, the agricultural produce of their farmer members. In the case of Kerala State Cooperative Marketing Federation Vs. Commissioner of Income-tax, the Hon'ble Supreme Court held that the use of words "or its members" in the relevant clause would mean the agricultural produce belonging to the members and not necessarily grown by them. Interpretation given to the use of the words in the provision is not in accordance with the legislative intent of the existing provision. In respect of income arising from transactions with non-members, the co-operatives are not different from other assessees, and such cooperatives are required to he taxed in the same manner as companies or other assessees engaged in marketing or agricultural produce. If an amendment in, section 80P(2)(6)(iii) was not made, it would have serious impact on revenues. The amendment, therefore, replaces the words "of its members" by the words "grown by its members". The amendment restricts the deduction to the profits derived by a cooperative society engaged in the marketing of agricultural produce grown by its members.

Central Ordinances, 1998-99

1. The National Institute of Pharmaceutical Education and Research (Second) Ordinance, 1998 (9 of 1998).
2. The Payment of Gratuity (Amendment) Ordinance, 1998 (110 of 1998).
3. The High Court and Supreme Court Judges (Conditions of Service) Amendment Ordinance, 1998 (11 of 1998).
4. The Representation of the People (Amendment) Ordinance, 1998 (12 of 1998).
5. The Essential Commodities (Amendment) Ordinance, 1998 (13 of 1998).
6. The Electricity Regulatory Commissions Ordinance, 1998 (14 of 1998).
7. The Central Vigilance Commission Ordinance, 1998 (15 of 1998).
8. The Prasar Bharati (Broadcasting Corporation of India) Amendment Ordinance, 1998 (16 of 1998).
9. The Oilfields (Regulation and Development) Amendment Ordinance, 1998 (17 of 1998).

10. The Central Vigilance Commission (Amendment) Ordinance. 1998 (18 of 1998).
11. The Companies (Amendment) Ordinance, 1998 (19 of 1998).
12. The Finance (No. 2) Amendment Ordinance, 1998 (20 of 1998).
13. The Companies (Amendment) Ordinance, 1999 (I of 1999).
14. The Prasar Bharati (Broadcasting Corporation of India) Amendment Ordinance, 1999 (2 of 1999).
15. The Patents (Amendment) Ordinance, 1999 (3 of 1999).
16. The Central Vigilance Commission Ordinance, 1999 (4 of 1999). -
17. The Urban Land (Ceiling and Regulation) Rcpeal Ordinance, 1999 (5 of 1999).
18. The Salary, Allowances and Pension of Members of Parliament (Amendment) Ordinance, 1999 (6 of 1999).

Subordinate legislation

During the period under review (1998), the number of Statutory Rules, Orders and Notifications vetted by this Department was 2,355.

Concurrent field legislation

The work relating to processing of Legislative proposals in respect of the following subjects hi the concurrent field (List III of the Seventh Schedule to die Constitution) has been allocated to this Department under the Government of India (Allocation of Business) Rules, 1961:-

(a) marriage and divorce, infants and minors, adoption, wills, intestacy and succession, joint family and partition;

(b) transfer of property other than agricultural land

(excluding benami transactions), registration 4 deeds and documents;

(c) contracts, but not including those relating agricultural land,

(d) actionable wrongs;

(e) bankruptcy and insolvency;

(f) trusts and trustees; Administrator General and Official trustees;

(g) evidence and oaths;

(h) civil procedure including limitation and arbitration; and

(i) charitable and religious endorsements and religious institutions.

Legislative proposals relating to the above subjects sponsored by the State Governments, and which, by virtue of the provisions of clause (2) of article 254 of the Constitution require assent of the President, are also scrutinised by this Department. During the calender year 1998, 85 references relating to State Bills/Ordinances were dealt with.

Training in legislative department

(i) The training facilities in the Legislative Drafting are available under the Commonwealth Fund for Technical Co-operation (C.F.T.C.) which offers such training facilities on regional basis to the countries in the Asian/African region. The training courses in the Legislative Drafting were introduced under the C.F.T.C. on the recommendation of the Conference of Law Ministers of the Commonwealth countries held in United Kingdom in 1973. The C.F.T.C. Programme for Training of Legislative Drafting has been in existence since 1974 and b-is conducted courses so far in different State Capitals including New Delhi, Colombo, Harare, Dhaka and Barbados.

Institute of legislative drafting and research

(ii) With a view to increasing the availability of trained legislative drafts person in the country, the Institute of Legislative Drafting and Research was established as a Wing of the Legislative Department, Ministry of Law and Justice in January, 1989. The Institute has been imparting theoretical as well as practical training in Legislative Drafting under four separate Courses, namely:

(a) Basic Course in Legislative Drafting of six months' duration for officers of the State Governments of Union territory Administrations;

(b) Advance Course of three months' duration for the senior level officers of the State Governments/Union territory Administrations;

(c) Refresher Course of short duration (iii the nature of a workshop) for the senior level officers of die State Governments/Union territory Administrations; and

(d) Appreciation Course of two weeks' duration for the officers of the various Central Government Ministries/Departments.

The institute also arranges awareness programme in Legislative Drafting for the benefit of Law students of various Universities visiting it.

Tenth basis course in legislative drafting

(iii) During the year, the Tenth Basic Course in Legislative Drafting was organised for a period of six months (i.e. from April, 1998 to September, 1998) for the benefit of the officers deputed by the State Governments/Union territory Administrations. An officer each from the States of Haryana, Kerala and Madhya Pradesh and two officers each from the States of Meghalaya, Nagaland and Sikkim and one officer from the Official Languages Wing of this Department (totalling ten officers) successfully completed the course.

Eighth appreciation course

(iv) The Eighth Appreciation Course meant for the Central Government officers of the level of Deputy Secretary, Under Secretary and Desk Officers/Section Officers was organised from the 9th November, 1998 to the 20th November, 1998. As regulations tinder various statutes are framed by the statutory bodies, the training was also extended to the officers of Public Sector Undertakings/ Subordinate offices under various Ministries/Departments of Government of India so as to enable them to learn drafting of such legislations, Eleven officers from different Ministries/Departments and one from a Public Sector Undertaking took part in the training programme.

Awareness programme

(v) The Institute arranged awareness programme in Legislative Drafting for the benefit of Law students from the University of Burdwan (West Bengal), who visited the Institute in September, 1998.

Imparting of practical training to foreign trainees of bureau of parliaamentary studies and training

(vi) The Bureau of Parliamentary Studies and Training, Lok Sabha Secretariat organises every year an International Training programme in Legislative Drafting of about two-and-a-half months' duration for various foreign Parliamentary/Government officials and officials of Parliament and State Legislature Secretariats of India with a view to equipping them with the basic concepts, skills and techniques, required for drafting of legislation so that they can render valuable assistance to the legislators when called upon to do so. As part of the said Training Programme, the Institute of Legislative Drafting and Research has been giving on-the-job practical training in the Legislative Drafting on an attachment basis. This year, the Bureau has ten trainee officers of foreign countries and one from the Parliament Secretariat and one from State Legislature Secretariats. The Institute has given on-the-job practical training to them from the 4th January, 1999 to the 15th January, 1999.

Computer-technology in the fielld of legisslation, etc.—India code on internet and nicnet

(vii) In house training programme in Computer operations has been conducted for the benefit of officers/staff of the Legislative Department for enabling them to progressively use Computer systems in their office work. All the Ordinances, Presidential Regulations and the Government Bills have been processed with the facilities now available on Computers.

India Code consists of unrepealed Central Acts of all-India application. The entire India Code has been made available on NICNET and INTERNET. The Department is acclimatising itself with the retrieval programme developed by the National Informatics Centra (NIC), Planning Commission, having data-base of the statute book and retrieval of Acts of Parliament for use in legislature drafting and up-dating the Acts of Parliament by carrying out their amendments. To have accurate text of the entire data relating to India Code, action is at hand in up-dating them in consultation with Government. The said retrieval system along with Home Page which is being up-dated from time to time is accessible on NICNET and INTERNET.

Issues relatingg to election laws

(i) Use of Electronic Voting Machines- The Electronic Voting Machine was used in 16 constituencies spread in the Union territory of Delhi add States of Madhaya Pradesh and Rajasthan during General Elections to their Legislative Assemblies held on 25.11.1998. The constituencies in the State of Madhya Pradesh where the Electronic Voting Machines were used were- 15-Gwalior, 16-Lashkar East, 17-Lashkar West, 239-Bhopal South and 240-Bhopal. North. In the State of Rajasthan, the constituencies where the Electronic Voting Machines were used were-41-Hazwamahal, 42-Johri Bazar, 43-Kishanpol, 95-Ajmer East (SC) and 96-Ajmer West and in Delhi-Sarojini Nagar, Gole Market, Minto Road, Kasturba Nagar, Jungpura and Delhi Cantonment were the constituencies where the Electronic Voting Machines were used. The performance of the Electronic Voting Machines was found to be satisfactory and their use was greatly appreciated by the public.

(ii) Proxy Voting for Members of the Armed Forces-The Election Laws (Amendment) Bill, 1998 was introduced in Lok Sabha on 22.12-1998 to provide that the members of the Armed Forces and Para-military Forces would have an additional option to vote by proxy. Earlier they had the option to either vote in person or through the postal ballot. The Election Commission of India, keeping in view the fact that with the enactment of the Representation of the People (Amendment) Act, 1996, the minimum campaign period has been reduced from 20 days to 14 days and keeping in view the logistic constraints involved in despatching postal ballots to members of the Armed Forces through their record offices and receiving those ballot papers back before counting process commences, recommended that the members of Armed Forces, in order to ensure their full participation in the electoral exercise, may be allowed to vote by proxy instead of postal ballot. The Government, accordingly, decided to provide an option to the members of the Armed Forces of the Union and Of Forces to which the provisions of the Army Act, 1950 have been made applicable, whether with or without modifications, to vote either in person or through the system of postal ballot or through the system of proxy, at an election in the manner to be specified in the rules.

Reservation of seats for women in the house of the people and the legislative assemblies of the states

(iii) The Constitution (Eighty-fourth Amendment) Bill,

1998 was introduced in Lok Sabha on 14.12.1998 to provide for one-third reservation of seats for women In Lok Sabha and Legislative Assemblies of the States.

Electoral reforms

(iv) The Representation of the People (Amendment) Act, 1998 was enacted to provide that, apart from local authorities, any institution, concern of undertaking established by or under a Central, Provincial or State Act, any company as defined in section 617 of the Companies Act, 1956 or any institution, concern or undertaking which is controlled or financed wholly or substantially by funds provided, directly or indirectly, by the Central Government or a State Government, shall make available their staff for election duties. The Act replaced the Representation of the People (Amendment) Ordinance, 1997 (Ord. 23 of 1997) which was repromulgated as the Representation of the People (Amendment) Ordinance, 1998 (Ord. 12 of 1998).

In addition, Government held a meeting with political parties on 22.5.1998 to discuss various proposals on electoral reforms and consequent upon a decision taken in that meeting, an 8-Member High Powered Committee under the Chairmanship of Shri Indrajit Gupta. Member of Parliament, was constituted to:—

(a) examine the pattern of State Funding in other countries where it is in vogue and suggest concrete proposals for providing State Funding to candidates set up by recognized political parties; and

(b) examine, in detail, the following related proposals and make suitable recommendations:

   (i) maintenance of accounts by political parties;

   (ii) ban on donation by companies to political parties;

   (iii) inclusion of expenses of political parties in the election expenses of candidates for purpose of ceiling on election expenses; and

(iv) empowering of the Election Commission of India to fix ceiling on election expenses before every General Election.

The Committee consisted of the following members:

(1) Shri Indrajit Gupta, M.P. (Chairman).

(2) Shri Somnath Chatterjee, M.P. (Member).

(3) Dr. Manmohan Singh, M.P. (Member).

(4) Shri V.K. Malhotra, M.P. (Member).

(5) Shri Madhukar Sarpotdar, M.P. (Member).

(6) Shri R. Muthiah, M.P. (Member).

(7) Shri Digvijay Singh, M.P. (Member).

(8) Prof. Ram Gopal Yadav, M.P. (Member).

The Committee has submitted its recommendations to the Government on 14th January, 1999. It has, inter alia, suggested partial State funding of elections, in kind, to the candidates set up by the recognised political parties.

Pursuant to another decision taken in the aforesaid meeting of political parties, Government has written to the Election Commission of India to review and reformulate the Model Code of Conduct, so reformulated, could be considered for giving statutory effect. In addition, the Election Commission of India has also been requested to review its order relating to Reservation and Allotment of Symbol hi consultation with political parties.

Sharing of election expenditure with state/union territory government

The entire expenditure on elections is initially met by the Governments of the concerned States and Union territories (with Legislatures) from the respective Consolidated Funds. The share of the Central Government in the expenditure is apportioned by Accountant Generals in accordance with principles mutually agreed upon between the Centre and the State Government/Union territory Administrations. According to these principles, the expenditure on preparation and printing of electoral rolls, election establishment and election material of common concern and Photo Identity Cards is shared equally between the Government of India and the State Governments/Union territory Administrations. The expenditure on the conduct of elections is also shared equally if the elections are held simultaneously to die Rouse of the People and Legislative Assemblies of the States or Union territories. The entire expenditure is borne by the Government of India in respect of election to the House of the People and by the State or Union territory Administrations in respect of election to the Legislative Assemblies. The entire election expenditure in respect of Union territories having no legislature is borne by the Government of India. Similarly, the entire expenditure on the conduct of elections to Rajya Sabha and to the offices of the President and the Vice President is also borne by the Government of India.

Modified edition of statutes

(i) The Department brings out from time to time modified edition of the Central Acts and some other important publications like Constitution of India, Manual of Election Law, Orders issued tinder the Constitution of India, etc. All the Central Laws up to the year 1958 have been compiled for bringing out in the form of Bharat Samhita (Revised edition of India Code) in diglot form, The Statement of Objects and Reasons appended to the principal Bills have also been added at the end of each Act included in the revised edition of India Code.

(ii) Volumes 1, II, IV, V. XI, XIII and XV of the revised edition of India Code have been published. Volumes III, VI, VII, VIII, IX, X, XII, XIV, XVI, XVII, XVIII, XIX, XX. XXI and XXII are under-print.

(iii) Annual Volumes of the Central Acts in book form for the years 1995 and 1996 have been printed and Annual Volume for the year 1997 is under-print.

(iv) The Constitution of India (pocket size) is under-print

(v) The Manual of Election. Law (revised edition) in diglot form has been printed.

(vi) Seven modified editions of the Central Acts have been published and six modified editions are under-print during the period tinder-report.

Public action of subordinate legislation under various acts

Pursuant to the recommendations of the Parliamentary Committee on Subordinate Legislation, a .scheme for maintaining Subordinate Legislation up-to-date and making the same available expeditiously to the public had been formulated. As subordinate legislation under an enactment is issued by the Ministry/ Department which is administratively concerned under the said scheme, the Administrative Ministries are required to maintain folders, containing up-to-date copies of all rules, orders and notifications issued by them. The Legislative Department, while preparing the revised edition of any Central Act, also independently compiles, on the basis of material available with it a manuscript of booklet containing all the subordinate legislation under the Act and sends the same to the Administrative Ministry concerned with the Act. The Administrative Ministry has to scrutinise the manuscript, finalise it and get it published. While the revised edition of an Act is published by the Legislative Department, the subordinate legislation under the Act is published by the Administrative Ministry.

Compilation of subordinate legislation under one Act, .has been published by the Administrative Ministry as companion volumes to the Act published by the

Legislative Department. Manuscript of subordinate legislation tinder three Acts are at an advanced stage of printing. Manuscripts of subordinate legislation tinder five Acts are under preparation in this Department, list of these are at ANNEXURE H.

Maintenance of central and state codes, etc.

Correction Section of Legislative Department is responsible for maintenance and up-dating of the Central Legislations, such as, India Code, Central Acts (not included in the India Code), Constitution of India, Manual of Election Law, General Statutory Rules and Orders, and for maintaining the Central Ordinances, Regulations, President's Acts and State Acts. The Section maintains Master copies of the India Code which, inter alia, contains unrepealed Central Acts for reference in the Ministry of Law, Justice and Company Affairs (Department of Legal Affairs and Legislative Department) and by the Ministers and other legal officers of the Government of India. These are valuable reference books.

Editing of manuscripts of bills, ordinances, etc.

The editing of manuscripts and checking proofs of Bills, Ordinances, Regulations, President's Bills, Adaptation Orders, Orders issued under the Constitution Of India, Delimitation of Council Constituencies Orders is done by the Printing Sections. Bills which are required to be introduced in a short time are also printed on behalf of the House of die People or the Council of States. Editing and proof-checking of the publications like the Constitution of India, Manual of Election Law, Revised edition of India Code, Annual Volume of Central Acts, Modified editions of Central Acts, Annual Reports, etc., are also done in these Sections. These Sections am also responsible for the publication of Central Acts, Ordinances, Regulations, President's Acts, etc., in the Gazette of India and their subsequent reprints as publications for sale.

Official Languages

The Official Languages Section of the Legislative Department is concerned with the over-all aspects of work relating to Official Language in the official work. This includes policy as also programme. This section processes proposals to secure authentication by the President of the translation of Central Acts in Hindi as well as regional languages before publication in the Official Gazette Approval for Hindi translation is required under section 5(l)(a) of the Official Languages Act, 1963 and for regional languages undersection 2(a) of the Authoritative Texts (Central Laws) Act, 1973. During the period from 1.4.1998 to 30.11.1998, the Section processed in all 34 Central Acts in Hindi and 58 in regional languages.

The Legislative Department has been declared as notified office on 29.4 1979 tinder rule 10(4) of the Official Languages (Use for Official Purposes of the Union) Rules 19%.

Official languages wing

Background and functions: During the national independence movement it was felt that only 'political freedom will not be sufficient to prove to the world that we are an independent Nation/State. An independent Nation/State is one which does not have to depend upon other languages (or the language of the foreign rulers) to manage its affairs: Keeping this in mind the Constituent Assembly adopted Hindi in Devenagari script as the Official Language of the country on the 14th September, 1949. With the enforcement of the Constitution on the 26th January, 1950 Hindi became the Official Language of the Union of India according to article 343 of the Constitution. On the recommendations of the Committee of Parliament on Official Language, the President issued an order to the Ministry of Law to constitute a Standing Commission legal experts. In pursuance of the directive issued by the

President, the Official Languages (Legislative) Commission was constituted in the year 1961.

Later on, the Government decided to departmentalise this work and put it on a permanent footing. With this objective the Commission was abolished and the Official Languages Wing was created as a pan of the Legislative Department. All those functions which were earlier assigned to the Commission have been entrusted to the Official Languages Wing besides some other functions. This was done with effect from the 1st October, 1976.

The principal functions assigned to the Official Language Wing or the Legislative Department are:

(i) to prepare and publish a standard legal terminology for use, as far as possible, in all official languages;

(ii) to prepare authoritative texts in Hindi of all Central Acts and Ordinances and Regulations promulgated by the President;

(iii) to prepare authoritative texts in Hindi of all Rules, Regulations and Orders made by the Central Government under any Central Act or Ordinance or Regulation promulgated by the President;

(iv) to prepare authoritative texts of all Central Acts and Ordinances and Regulations promulgated by the President in the respective official languages of the States and to arrange for the translation of all Acts passed and Ordinances promulgated in any State into Hindi, if the texts of such Acts or Ordinances are in a language other than Hindi;

(v) to perform such other duties as may be assigned to it by the Government of India from time to time.

Subsequently following functions have also been added:

(1) Translation in Hindi of deeds, legal documents like contracts, agreements, leases, bonds, mortgages, etc;

(2) Translation into Hindi of all statutory Notifications under section 3(3) of the Official Languages Act, 1963;

(3) Translation into Hindi of Statutory Rules issued by Governments of non-Hindi Waking States for being laid before Parliament when such State-, are under Presidential rule;

(4) Translation into Hindi of all the Parliament Questions/Answers, Assurances, etc., relating to the Ministry of Law, Justice and Company Affairs;

(5) Training in Legislative Drafting in Hindi to officers from Hindi speaking States;

(6) Work relating to Coordinating Committee of Hindi speaking States for ensuring effective coordination in the evolution of uniform legal phraseology and model of standard clauses in Hindi and publication thereof,

(7) Work relating to Hindi Salhakar Samiti of the Ministry of Law, Justice and Company Affairs and providing Grants-in-Aid to Voluntary organizations for promotion of Official Language in the field of law;

(8) Publication of diglot editions of Central Acts also been added at the end of each Act included it, the (with legislative history) and popularisation thereof; revised edition of India Code.

(9) Preparation and maintenance of India Code in Hindi (Bharat Sanhita) and also in diglot form;

(10) Publication of regional languages versions of the Constitution of India and arranging functions for the release thereof.

Legal glossary

The work of developing and publishing "Legal Glossary" is a continuous process. Since the inception of Official Languages (Legislative) Commission in 1961 five editions of Legal Glossary have been brought out and every successive edition was larger in size. While the first edition

(1970) contained 20,000 entries, the fifth edition (1992) of Legal Glossary contained 61,000 entries spread over in seven parts. The Legal Glossary brought out by the Official Languages Wing has received wide acclaim by discerning men of law and letters. Work on bringing out another enlarged edition of Legal Glossary has already been started.

Constitution of India

The diglot edition of the Constitution of India was first published in 1988. The second edition of the same was published in 1990. The third edition of the Constitution of India was brought up-to-date in 1991. A supplement to the Constitution of India in diglot form had also been brought out in 1994 containing the Constitution (Sixty-ninth Amendment) Act, 1991 to the Constitution (Seventy-fifth Amendment) Act, 1993. In 1996 another edition of' the diglot version was brought out incorporating all the amendments up to and including the Constitution (Seventy-eighth Amendment) Act, 19(5. A separate edition of the Constitution of India in A-4 size has already been published and pocket size of the same is in the process of printing.

Bharat samhita

All the Central Laws have been compiled and brought out in the form of India Code in handy-volumes. The last edition of India Code consisting of eight Volumes was published in 1959. Action has already been initiated for bringing out Bharat Samhita (Revised Edition of India Code) in diglot form. This will consist of about 60 volumes and will contain Hindi and English versions of Central Acts of general importance in chronological order. One of the salient features of these Codes will be that the Statement of Objects and Reasons appended to the principal Bill has also been added at the end of each Act included in the revised edition of India Code.

Volumes I, II, IV, V, XI, XIII and XV of the revised edition of India Code have already been published by Official Languages Wing. Volumes HI, VI, VII, VIII, IX, X, XII, XIV, XVI, XVIII, XIX and XX are at the different stages of printing.

Preparation and publication of authoritative texts of central acts

As mentioned earlier, the task of publication of authoritative texts of Central Acts in Hindi devolved on the Official Languages Wing. During the period tinder report, 49 Acts have been published in the Official Gazette as authoritative texts thereof in the Hindi language under section 5(l)(a) of the Official Languages Act, 1963, total number of such Acts have gone up to 1,765.

Preparation and publication of authorised translation of president's acts, ordinances and regulations

The Hindi version of 27 Ordinances, 7 Notes for the Cabinet consisting of 394 pages were also prepared by this Wing.

Constitution orders

The Hindi version of all the Constitution Orders, which were issued during the said period, have also been prepared by this Wing.

Publication of diglot editions of central acts

Central Acts, for which there is a likelihood of public demand, are published by the Official Languages Wing in diglot form. During the year, 1998, four such Acts have been printed so far. Out of these, one Act has been printed for the first time and three Acts have been printed twice and even more.

Authorised hindi translation of bills

Sub-section (2) of section 5 of the Official Languages Act, 1963 which was brought into force on the 1st October, 1976, required that all Bills to be introduced or amendments thereto moved in either House of Parliament shall be accompanied by translation of the same in Hindi. During the period under review, the Hindi version of 71 Bills comprising 1,751 pages was supplied to both the Houses of Parliament.

Central statutory rules and orders (G.S.R.O.'s)

Sub-section (3) of section 3 of the Official Languages Act, 1963 is a very important provision. It lays down the foundation for bilingual working of the Central Government. Under clause (i) of that subsection, all resolutions, general orders, rules i notifications, etc., is tied or made by the Central Government must be both in Hindi and English languages. The Official Languages Wing of the Legislative Department has been entrusted with the job of preparation of such statutory rules and orders, etc., in Hindi for simultaneous publication in the Official Gazette. It may be noted that no notification can be published in the Gazette of India in English alone. It has to be published in English and Hindi and that too simultaneously. During the period under report the number of pages of such rules, notifications, etc., were 8.051.

Preparation and publication of authoritative text of rules, regulations, orders, etc.

Clause (b) of sub-section (1) of section 5 of the Official Languages Act, 1963 requires that a translation in. Hindi published under the authority of the President in the Official Gazette of any order, rule, regulation or bye-law issued under the Constitution or under any Central Act shall be deemed to he the authoritative text thereof in Hindi. Up to December, 1998, the Official Languages Wing has prepared the translation of 802 ,such rules, regulations, orders, etc., in Hindi. Out of them, the authoritative texts of 798 rules, etc., have been published in the Official Gazette.

Preparation and publiccation of subordinate legilsation in diglot form

Persuant to the recommendations of the Committee on Subordinate Legislation, a scheme for Preparation of Subordinate Legislation and making the same available to the public has been formulated by the Government. A subordinate legislation under an enactment is issued by the Ministry or Department, which is administratively concerned, the Official Languages Wing prepares and sends the Hindi version of such subordinate legislation which is required by the Administrative Ministries or Departments for publication in diglot form. Some of such compilations of subordinate legislation have been published by the Administrative Ministries or Departments as companion volumes to the Act, e.g., the Income-tax Manual, the Wealth-tax Manual, the Gift-tax Manual, the Estate Dpty Manual, the Companies (Profits) Surtax Manual, compilation of Fundamental Rules and Supplementary Rules, compilation of Railway Services (Pension) Rules, compilation of Rail Road Tariff Rules, etc.

The Official Languages Wing, while preparing the revised edition of the Central Acts, which are of public Importance, also independently compiles on die material available with it, the manuscripts of diglot edition of the Act containing subordinate legislation under that Act. The few names of such Acts are:

(1) The Official Languages Act, 1963.

(2) The Dowry Prohibition Act, 1961.

(3) The Presidential and Vice-Presidential Elections Act, 1952.

(4) The Food Adulteration Act, 1954.

(5) The Citizenship Act, 1955.

Maintenance of ccentral codes, etc.

The Correction Section of the Official Languages Wing

maintaining 18 sets of India Code as well as Bharat Samhita. Besides, it also keeps other important manuals up-to-date for reference by officers in this Wing. Apart from this, this Section also maintains different parts of the Central Gazette for ready reference. This Section has also prepared up-to-date Hindi version of Volumes XX, XXI, XXII of India Code for publication in diglot form. The work of preparing Hindi manuscript of Volume XXIII of India Code in diglot form is at hand.

In addition, this Section

(a) also supplied up-to-date copies of about 89 Central Acts to various State Governments for translation into various regional languages;

(b) has also distributed the Gazette copies of Hindi version of 9 Central Acts to Hindi speaking States for publication in their State Gazettes.

Editing of manuscripts, bills, acts, ordinances, diglot edititions, etc., and publication thereof

The Printing Section of the Official Languages Wing is primarily concerned with the editing of manuscripts and checking of proofs of Bills, Ordinances, Regulations, President's Acts, etc., issued under the Constitution of India, Delimitation of Council Constituencies Orders, etc. Bills which are required to be introduced in a short time are also printed on behalf of the House of the People or the: Council of States. Editing and proof-checking of the publication in diglot form of the Constitution of India. Manual of election Law, Revised Edition of India Code, modified diglot edition of Central Acts, Statutory Rules and Orders. Annual Reports, etc., ate also done in this Section. This section is also responsible for the printing and publication of Central Acts, Ordinances, Regulations, President's Acts, etc., and their subsequent reprints in diglot form as publications for sale. This section discharged all its responsibilities during the year under review.

In addition to the aforesaid work, the Printing Section of the Official Languages Wing is also performing the duties of the Publication Section.

Preparation and publication of standard legal documents
The Official Languages Wing of the Legislative Department is meant for the translation of statutory material of Government Departments and Offices. However, the section 3(3)(iii) of the Official Languages Act, 1963 requires that both Hindi and English languages are to be used for agreements, contracts, leases, bonds, tenders, etc., in order to facilitate compliance with the requirements of the said Act, the Official Languages Wing prepares for various Ministries and Departments of the Central Government, the Hindi version of such documents, with a view to achieve uniformity in the translation of Standard Legal Documents in use by the Central Government Offices. This Wing has prepared and published eight volumes of the repeatedly used legal documents in diglot form till date These volumes have rendered sufficient assistance in the use of Official Languages, Hindi., These compilations were received well, not only by various Departments/Ministries but also by the Government Undertakings and State Governments.

The Official languages Wing also prepares for the day-to-day use of various Departments of the Central Government, the Hindi version of such documents. During the period under report, the Hindi version of 1206 pages of Parliament Questions/Answers/Assurances of this Ministry and such Documents have been supplied to different Ministries/Departments.

Establishing the Indian languages in the sphere of law
The Official Languages Wing is constantly doing and/or getting done the work of translation of Central Acts into Hindi and other languages. So far as the Regional Languages are concerned, this work is being done with

the cooperation and consent of die various State Governments. Regarding these languages, this work is being done in a planned way by preparing the list of important Central Acts.

Apart from Hindi language, the Official Languages Wing has so far published the Constitution of India in thirteen other languages, namely, Assamese, Bengali, Gujarati, Kannada, Malayalam, Marathi, Oriya, Punjabi, Sanskrit, Tamil, Telugu, Urdu and Sindhi. More than one edition of most of these versions have been published and in case of Marathi, fourth edition was brought out in 1992.

By the Constitution (Seventy-first Amendment) Act, 1992, the Konkani, Manipuri and Nepali languages have been inserted in the Eighth Schedule to the Constitution of India. Efforts are being made to bring out the Konkani, Manipuri and Nepali version of the constitution.

The Official Languages Wing also published the authoritative texts of Central Acts in regional languages as, envisaged under section 2 of the Authoritative Texts (Central Laws) Act, 1973 (50 of 1973). The progress of translation work of the Central Acts in regional languages during the year under report is reflect-A in the table below:

S. No.	Name of the Language	Translation of Acts approved by O.L. Wing	No. of Acts authenticated as Authoritative Texts
1.	Assamese	08	–
2.	Bengali	–	01
3.	Gujarati	05	33
4.	Kannada	11	06
5.	Malayalam	04	04
6.	Marathi	09	13
7.	Oriya	12	–
8.	Punjabi	–	01
9.	Tamil	–	41
10.	Telugu	06	01
11.	Urdu	13	–
	Total	68	100

Wide distribution of central acts, leggal glossary, etc.

This year also the Official Languages Wing has .sent to all Hindi speaking States, Gujarat and Maharashtra as also High Courts in these States, concerned Ministries/ Departments of Government of India, Andaman and Nicobar Islands, the Nagri Pracharini Sabha, Parliament Library and other libraries, the Gazette copies of Hindi version of Central Acts after they have been authenticated and published in the Gazette of India. Copies of the Central Acts in diglot form are regularly sent to all States (Hindi as well as non-Hindi speaking States), Supreme Court of India, Parliament library and all High Courts.

As per requirement, the copies of the last edition of the Legal Glossary have been distributed to all officials of the Legislative Department including the various Ministries, Departments, Parliament library, Courts, Official Languages Commissions/Committees of the States, Vidhi Sahitya Prakashan, Government Undertakings, etc.

Work relating to the hindi salahakar samiti

In pursuance of the Legislative Department's Resolution, the Government of India re-constituted the Hindi Salahkar Samiti for the Ministry of Law and Justice on 18th June, 1997. The new committee consists of members from the Lok Sabha and members from the Raiya Sabha. Besides, the committee also includes about nineteen other non-official members and invites.

The function of the Samiti is normally to advise the Central Government on matters relating to-

(i) the translation of Central Acts and statutory rules into Hindi-,

(ii) the evolution of common legal terminology;

(iii) the Production of the standard law books in Hindi, for imparting legal education in Hindi in law colleges and universities;

(iv) the publication of law journals and reports in Hindi; and

(v) the matters ancillary and incidental to any of the above items.

The last meeting of the newly constituted committee was held on 15.09.1997 under the Chairmanship of the then Minister of State for Law and Justice Shri Ramakant D. Khalap.

Grants-in-aid to voluntary organisations

There is a scheme for the propagation and development of Hindi and other Indian languages in the field of law. According to which the voluntary organisations and institutions are provided with financial aid. Since !985, the Official Languages Wing is implementing such scheme to give financial aid to those voluntary organisations which undertake publication of law books or journals in Hindi and other regional languages,

With a view to ensuring the compliance of the recommendation of the Hindi Salahkar Samiti, a high powered committee for Financial Assistance to voluntary organisations had been constituted on the 3rd May, 1995. The tenure of the committee expired on the 2nd May, 1998. Proposal for constituting new committee has been submitted and it is expected that it will be approved soon.

Vidhi sahitya prakashan

(i) In the year 1958, the Committee of Parliament on Official Languages had recommended that arrangements be made early to bring out authorised translations of important judgments of the Hon'ble Supreme Court and the Hon'ble High Courts in India arid this work could be entrusted to a Central Office in Delhi working under the supervision of Law Departmental Thereafter, on the recommendation of the Hindi Advisory Committee, a Journal Wing was set up in the Ministry of Law and Justice in 1968 with the objective of promoting the use of

Hindi in the legal field. This Wing was subsequently redesignated as "VIDHI SAHITYA PRAKASHAN".

Initially, a monthly publication of all the judgments of Supreme Court of India, as marked 'REPORTABLE' by the bench of the Court, delivering the judgment concerned, ccommenced in April, 1968 and it was designed as "Uchchatama Nyayalaya Nirnaya Patrika". Another publication containing judgment of all the High Courts of India was started in January, 1969 and it was designated as "Uchcha Nyayalaya Nirnaya Patrika". In 1987 Uchcha Nyayalaya Nirnaya Patrika was bifurcated into two Patrikas, i.e. Uchcha Nyayalaya Civil Nirnaya Patrika and Uchcha Nyayalaya Dandik Nirnaya Patrika contains selected reportable judgments of the Supreme Court and the Uchcha Nyayalaya Civil Nirnaya Patrika and Uchcha Nyayalaya Dandik Nirnaya Patrika contains selected judgments of civil and criminal cases of all the High Courts respectively. These are being published monthly and the number of Royal Octari size of pages per month on an average has been for these Patrikas are 700. Due to phenomenal increase in the volume of the reportable judgements of the Hon'ble Supreme Court, the strength of the Hon'ble Supreme Court Judges rose from 9 in 1988 to 26 and failure to increase the strength of the editorial as well as the other requisite staff of the V.S.P, the Ministry of Law, Justice and Company Affairs in the Legislative Department decided that only very very important and scrupulously selected of the Hon'ble High Courts shall be Digests based on these Patrikas are also published from time to time.

A quarterly journal entitled "Vidhi Sahitya Samachar', is also twing published which contained detailed information regarding various activities in the field of law and publications of Vidhi Sahitya Prakashan. A 'Publication List' containing priced publications of Vidhi

Sahitya Prakashan is also made available to the customers from time to time.

Apart from the publication of the above three Patrikas, the Vidhi Sahitya Prakashan is also in charge of the following works, namely:—

(a) publication of Law Test Books in Hindi for use in the academic field and as reference books;

(b) translation of legal classics in Hindi,

(c) awarding of various prizes for the best publications in the field of law;

(d) sale of Hindi publications of Vidhi Sahitya Prakashan and Official Languages Wing of the Ministry of Law, Justice and Company Affairs in the Legislative Department; and

(e) holding of conferences, seminars and exhibitions at different important places in India, particularly in Hindi speaking States for popularisation and improvement of legal literature in Hindi.

In addition, standard law books in Hindi written by eminent authors arc also being published by the Vidhi Sahitya Prakashan for the use of law students, law teachers, lawyers and judicial officers. In order to give incentive to authors and publishers, in the private sector, prizes am awarded annually for the best publications in Hindi, in the field of law Seminars, in law colleges, District Courts, High Courts and Law Departments of the State. Governments of the Hindi speaking States are held for the propagation and development of Hindi in die field of law. Vidhi Sahitya Prakshan also holds exhibitions of its publications and publications of the Official Languages Wing in different Hindi Speaking States. It also looks after the sale of its publications as well ais the sale of diglot (English-Hindi) Central Acts.

The details of achievements made during the year under consideration are set out item-wise in short hereinafter.

Publication of nirnaya patrikas: During the year 1998-99 four issues of Uchcha Nyayalaya Civil Nirnaya Patrikas and three issues of Uchcha Nyayalaya Dandik Nirnaya Patrika were published.

Introduction of computer printing technology: During die year 1998-99 it was decided that issues of judgments of Supreme Court of India and various High Courts should be prepared on floppies. The new system of computers were installed and Stenographers have been trained by National Informatics Centre (NIC). Though it took time to get familiar with the new system. It is now being done regularly.

During the year 1998-99, the manuscript of the 35 issues of Uchchatama Nyayalaya Nirnaya Patrikas have been sent to press. Various issues of Uchcha Nyayalaya Dandik Nirnaya Patrika since 1993 to 1996 are in various stages of printing. A floppy for November, 1996 issue have been prepared and sent to the press for printing. Similarly, various issues of Uchcha Nyayalaya Civil Nirnaya Patrika from July 93 to December, 93 October, 94 to Dec. 94 and January, 95 to December, 1996 are lying in various stages of printing Floppies of the issues of February, 1997 to May, 1997 have been prepared and sent to the press for printing.

Indices: All the four quarterly indices of Uchchatama Nyayalaya Nirnaya Patrika for the year 1994 have been published Part I of the Uchcha Nyayalaya Dandik Nirnaya Patrika for the year 1993 have been published and Part I (Half yearly) Uchcha Nyayalaya Civil Nirnaya Patrika for the year 1993 have been published.

Subscribers of the patrikas for 1997-98: During the year under review, the number of the subscribers of the Patrikas was as tinder—

Name of the Patrika	No. of Subscribers
Uchchatama Nyayalaya Nirnaya Patrika	776
Uchcha Nyayalaya Civil Nirnaya Patrika	776
Uchcha Nyayalaya Dandik Nirnaya Patrika	776
Vidhi Sahitya Samachar	95

Digest: Five years (1988-92) Digest of Uchchtama Nyayalaya Nirnaya Patrika, three years' (1990-92) Digest of Uchcha Nyayalaya Dandik Nirnaya Patrika and three years' Digest (1990-92) of Uchcha Nyayalaya Civil Nirnaya Patrika have been printed and their price is yet to be fixed by the Ministry.

Award of prizes: The Evaluation Committee for the award of prizes under the Scheme has been reconstituted w.e.f. 26th August, 1997 and during the year 1998-99, awards for the Years 1995, 1996 and 1997 have been decided. Besides an author to write Hindi book on Jurisprudence have been recommended. Hindi book on Jurisprudence have been recommended. Hindu Vidhi Ke Siddhant, a book published by the Ministry have been adjudged the best book of the decade (1983-92). Awards for the books have been increased from Rs. 10,000 to Rs. 25,000/-, Similarly, awards for the Hindi books, received from the private sector have been increased.

Books: So far 29 Standard law books in Hindi have been published. Print order namely Audhunik Parivarik Vidhi & Bhartiya Dand sanhita have been given for printing and revised and enlarged editions of four books namely Shram Vidhi (Labour Law), Vidhik Upchar (Legal Remedies), Hindu Vidhi (Hindu Law) and Chikitsa Nyayashastra aur Vish-Vigyan (Medical Jurisprudence and Taxocology) are in the final stages of the printing. The third revised editions of "Prashasnik Vidhi" and "Sampatti Antaran Adhiniyam" have been edited and is being sent to Press for printing. The third revised editions of Dand Prakriya Sanhita and Bhagidari Adhiniyam are being prepared.

3

Department of Justice

Supreme Court

The authorised strength of the Supreme Court Judges (including the Chief Justice of India) is 26. There were four vacancies in the apex court as on 10th December, 1998.

High courts

(i) The Government of India have adopted a policy of having Chief Justices of High Courts from outside the States over which the Courts have jurisdiction. During the year under review two Chief Justices were appointed/ transferred in the High Courts under this policy. High Courts of Allahabad, Andhra Pradesh, Bombay, Calcutta, Delhi, Gauhati, Rajasthan and Sikkim have acting Chief Justices.

(ii) As on 10-12-1998, the total sanctioned strength of Judges and Additional Judges of the various High Courts was 587. In addition, posts of 6 permanent Judges and 25 Additional Judges would be created in different High Courts.

(iii) Four fresh appointments of Judges/Additional Judges were made in the High Courts and in addition 26 Additional Judges were appointed as permanent Judges during April-December 10, 1998. The details of appointment of thew Judges are indicated below:

S. No	High Court	Initial appoint-ments	Additional Judges made permanent
1.	Andhra Pradesh	01	01
2.	Bombay	–	10
3.	Delhi	–	01
4.	Gauhati	01	01
5.	Gujarat	–	04
6.	Karnataka	02	03
7.	Orissa	–	01
8.	Punjab & Haryana	–	01
9.	Rajasthan	–	04
	Total	04	26

(iv) As on 10-12-1998, there were 161 vacancies in Various High Courts.

(v) No Audit Report is pending.

Plan funds for the judiciary

A Centrally Sponsored Scheme relating to development of infrastructural facilities for the judiciary is being implemented by the Department of Justice from the year 1993-94. The Scheme is being implemented with a view to augment the resources of the State Governments/Union territories Administrations. The Scheme includes construction of court buildings, and residential accommodation for Judges/Judicial Officers covering High Courts and Subordinate Courts. The expenditure under the Scheme is shared by the Central and State Governments. on 50:50 basis. The expenditure in respect of Union territories is met fully by the Centre.

From 1993-94 to 1997-98, an amount of rupees 232.43 crores has been released to various States/Union territories. An expenditure of Rupees 482.81 crores has been incurred on various permissible works under the scheme till Match, 1998. For the year 1998-99, a budget provision of Rupees 52 crores has been made for implementing the scheme. Out of this, the first instalment of Rs. 21.54 crore has been released to various States/UTs.

National judicial academy

(i) National Judicial Academy (NJA) has been established by the Government of India for providing in-service training to judicial officers. The Academy is run by an autonomous body registered under the Societies Registration Act, 1860 (Act XXI of 1860). The NJA is registered with Registrar of Societies, Delhi on 17-08-1993 and it came into existence w.e.f. that date.

(ii) The management of the society is entrusted to Governing Council under the Chairmanship of the Chief Justice of India. "Two other Judges of the Supreme

Court of India, Secretaries to the Government of India in the Department of Justice, Department of Legal Affairs and Department of Expenditure are its other members. The Registrar General, Supreme Court of India is the Member Secretary of the Governing Council. The NJA is located at Bhopal in Madhya Pradesh with its registered office in the Supreme Court premises at New Delhi. The building complex of the Academy is already under construction at Bhopal for which the Government has approved an amount of Rs. 48.04 crores. A certain portion of the fund under the Centrally Sponsored Scheme relating to infrastructural facilities for the judiciary is set aside for meeting the expenses of the NJA in consultation with the Planning Commission. Till the end of the financial year 1997-98, an amount of Rs. 20.53 crores has been released to the Academy to meet its expenses. For the current financial year i.e. 1998-99, an amount of Rs. 18 crores has been allocated for the Academy, of which an amount of Rs. 9 crores has been released till November, 1998.

(iii) The progress of the construction work of the Academy is being closely monitored and it is felt that the construction of the Academy will be completed within the scheduled time i.e. by December, 1999.

(iv) Despite the fact that the Academy is not yet fully functional, it has already carried out a number of academic activities. The Academy organised a training programme on "Gender and Law" for the second batch of 10 judicial officers from different States/High Courts in collaboration with the British Council Division. These officers underwent 6 weeks' training at the Warwichsher University, United Kingdom, under the Colombo Plan. The Academy also organised 2 regional seminars at Lucknow and Hyderabad to disseminate the outputs of die "Gender and Law" project. In future also the Academy proposes to organise similar orientation courses and seminars with the help of the regional institutes to cover more region and more judicial officers.

First national judicial pay commission

The First National Judicial Pay Commission has been set up under the Chairmanship of Shri Justice K.J. Shetty, a retired judge of the Supreme Court vide resolution dated 21-3-96; in compliance with a direction of the Supreme Court of India in Writ Petition No. 1022/1989- All India Judges Association Vs. Union of India. Its terms of reference include examinations and recommendations in respect of salary, allowances and other conditions of service of the members of subordinate judiciary of the entire country. The Commission will also make recommendations regarding minimum qualifications, age, method of recruitment, work environment, etc., for the judicial Officers. It will submit its report to the State Governments as the Judicial Officers are the employees of the respective State Governments. The Commission is already in the midst of its work. It has already recommended the grant of interim relief to the Judicial Officers.

Revision of salary and pension of the judges

(i) On the basis of the recommendations of the Fifth Central Pay Commission, the salary of the Judges of the Supreme Court and the High Courts has been revised with effect from 1-1-1996 through the High Court and Supreme Court Judges (Conditions of Service) Amendment Act, 1998 (Act No. 18 of 1998).

(ii) The revised salaries of the Judges w.e.f. 1-1-1996 are as follows:

Chief Justice of India	Rs. 33,000/- per month
Judges of Supreme Court	Rs. 30,000/- per month
Chief Justices of High Courts	Rs. 30,000/- per month
Judges of High Courts	Rs. 26,0001- per month

(iii) The pension, additional pension and family pension of the Judges are slated to be revised with effect from 01-01-1996 through the High Court and Supreme Court Judges (Salaries and Conditions of Service) Amendment Act, 1998. This Act also proposed to raise the House Rent Allowance (HRA) of a Judge of the Supreme Court and the High Court to Rs. 10,000/- per month at a flat rate.

4

General

Deputations/delegations abroad

From 1st April, 1998 to 30th November, 1998:
(1)Shri D. P. Sharma, Joint Secretary and Legal Adviser, visited Paris (France) during 1-3 April, 1998 to finalise Indo-French Extradition Treaty.

(2) Dr. S.S. Chahar, Deputy Legal Adviser visited Geneva during 27-29 April, 1998 in connection with Oral Hearing before W.T.O.

(3) Shri A. P. Agarwal, Additional Legal Adviser visited Sri Lanka During 15-19 June, 1998 to participate in the Commonwelth Workshop on Legal Implemetation of the WTO Agreement.

(4) Shri K.D. Singh, Joint Secretary and Legal Adviser visited Tokyo during 5-7 October, 1998 to participate in the meeting of Asian Regional Forum on Intellectual Property Policy Development Orgainsed by WIPO.

(5) Shri R. L. Meena, Law Secretary visited Vienna during 6-8 October, 1998 to participate in the meeting of Expert Group of UNCITRAL.

(6) Shri D.R. Meena, Joint Secretary and Legal Adviser visited Bulgaria during 12-13 October, 1998 to participate in the discussion on Exrtradition. Treaty.

(7) Shri V. V. Singh Legal Adviser (Conveyancing) visited U.K. France and Netherland during 9-12 November, 1998 to participate in the negotiation of JPY 8.885 billion re-financing loan through syndication the Indian Railway Finance Corporation Ltd.

(8) Shri R.L. Koli, Joint Secretary and Legal Adviser visited Saudi Arabia and Qatar during 24-30 November, 1998 in connection with BIPA negotiation.

(9) Shri A. Sinha, Joint Secretary and Legal Adviser visited Singapore during 28-30 November, 1998 for re-financing existing UYon loan availed from Exim Bank of Japan in 1988.

(10) Dr. Raghbir Singh, Secretary, Legislative Department attended the Academi Session of world Intellectual Property Organisation held at Geneva from.

(11) Dr. Sanjay Singh, Deputy Legislative Counsel, Legislative Department attended the Training Cow-se in U.K. under the Colombo Plan from 4-3-1998 to 2805-1998 in London.

Reservation for scheduled castes, scheduled tribes, ex-servicemen and physically handicapped persons

(i) There are arrangements in the Department of Legal Affairs and in the Legislative Department to ensure compliance with the Government's order relating to reservation in services for the Scheduled Castes and the Scheduled Tribes.

(ii) A cell under the direct control of the liaison officer of the level of Deputy Secretary is functioning in the Department of Legal Affairs, to ensure strict enforcement of the Orders/Instructions of the Government of India, relating to reservation in service for Scheduled Castes/ Scheduled Tribes and other Backward Classes. Another liaison officer of the level of Deputy Registrar is also functioning in the Income tax Appellate Tribunal for strict enforcement of reservation orders in the Tribunal. This arrangement is working satisfactorily.

(iii) There are three liaison officers in the three Administrative Units of the Legislative Department, viz.- Legislative Department (Main), Vidhi Sahitya Prakashan and Principal Accounts Office to oversee the implementation of Orders/Instructions of the Government on reservation for Scheduled Castes/Scheduled Tribes and Ex-Servicemen and Physically Handicapped persons in service/posts in the respective units.

(iv) A statement showing the total number of employees in the Department of Legal Affairs and Legislative Department and the number of Scheduled Castes/Scheduled Tribes and the Ex-Servicemen amongst them as on 1.1.1998 and the another statement showing the particulars of recruitment made during the year and the number of the posts filled by candidates belonging to the Scheduled Castes/Scheduled Tribes are enclosed.

Departmental accounting organisation

(i) The Accounting Organisation of Ministry of Law and Justice is entrusted with the responsibility of making timely payment, of personal claims like Salary, Travel Expenses, Office Contingency and Rate, Rent and Taxes, etc. During the period under report the personal claims including loans and advances to Government servants, withdrawal from in G.P.F. etc., were settled promptly. Payments of grants-in-aid to the various Bodies/ institutions of Centre and States were made on top priority basis. The Central Government share's of Election were also dealt with quickly to pass on the credit to the concerned States through Reserve Bank of India, CAS, Nagpur. While processing the claims and other payments it was ensured that payments are made in accordance with the rules, orders and provisions in force on the subjects and no fraudulent/over payments are made. It was generally observed that expenditure on these account should not be exceeded the Budget allotment. Prompt action has been taken to intimate the figures of receipt and expenditure incurred by various units to the concerned Departmental Officers so as to provide an opportunity to them to reconcile the figures of that office with the figures of concerned Pay and Accounts Office during the period of report. All necessary efforts are being made to maintain the ledger and broadsheets for these payments so as to ensure that every expenditure that has been accounted for in the books and gives clear and accurate picture.

Pensionary benefits

(ii) This Organisation is responsible for providing pensionary benefits to the retired employees by granting pensions and gratuity and other retirement benefits. All the cases of pensions were dealt with on top priority basis and no delay was reported by any Government employee for sanctioning of pension, gratuity and other retirement benefits. This office has assisted the Departmental Officers by way of giving the advice on the matters regarding the pensionary benefits referred to this Organisation from time to time. Most of the cases received for revision of pension/ family pension consequent upon recommendations of fifth pay commission have been settled and remaining cases are under process in consultation with appropriate Administrative Authorities.

General provident fund

(iii) As is required under the provisions of Government's rule, the General Provident Fund Statement showing the total credits and debits of fund in the accounts of the subscribers including the interest on the principal has been sent to them on the due date, i.e., 15th July each year and in the case of merged DDO by 31st May each year. Broadsheets; and ledgers maintained for the reconciliation of figures in respect of General Provident Fund were also regularly closed. All the cases of final withdrawal of General Provident Fund on retirement or otherwise were decided on top priority basis and payment made to the subscribers immediately on their retirement without any delay.

Accounts at a glance

(iv) In order to take the effective control over the expenditure, the Accounting Organisation prepares Accounts at a Glance on yearly basis to bring out the flow of expenditure for the information of the higher authorities so that advance action can be taken for the procurement of additional fund in the Revised Estimates for new services of plans. This account also facilitates the higher authorities to take into account the required receipt and expenditure to consider the various plants to be implemented and to provide the funds for various bodies/ institutions in shape of grants-in-aid. The flow of expenditure during the past year is shown to instruct the Departmental Officers to monitor the expenditure according to the instructions issued by the Ministry of Finance from time to time.

This unit also submits the monthly accounts well in time to Controller General of Accounts, Ministry of Finance, Department of Expenditure depicting the exact state of affairs of the receipt and expenditure of this Ministry including the amount lying outstanding under the various Suspense Heads such as Public Sector Bank Suspense and PAO Suspense. This Organisation has I charged' expenditure of Supreme Court of India and this office also maintains the accounts of charged expenditure. The compilation of accounts were carried out on top priority basis. All efforts are being made to 'reduce the outstanding balance under the various Suspense Heads and adverse balances, if any.

Appropriation accounts, statement of central transactions and finance accounts

(v) The Accounting Organisation of the Ministry of Law and Justice is required to prepare the Annual

Appropriation Accounts, Statement of Central Transaction and Finance Accounts comprising details 5. Introduction of Award Scheme for Central of transactions of Ministry of Law and Justice and Government Employees as well as Members of General Supreme Court of India. All the three reports for the year 1997-98 are prepared on due dates and were furnished to Controller General of Accounts, Ministry 6. Introduction of Scheme for grant of Cash Awards of Finance, Department of Expenditure and Director General of Audit, Central Revenues after getting activities approved from all the three Chief Accounting Authorities, i.e., Law Secretary, Secretary Legislative Department and Registrar General of Supreme Court of India.

Internal audit

(vi) Out of 49 units, 40 units are due for audit in the current year 1998-99 (9 are biannual and not due during the current year). A significant work has been done by the Internal Audit Wing by concluding 23 units, on the date, remaining 17 units (10 outstation and 7 at Delhi) are still outstanding which could not be concluded as entire Internal Audit wing has been directed to complete Pay Fixation cases as per direction of Controller General of Accounts in various offices/Departments under Ministry of Law and Justice through out country. Balance 7, local units would be completed up to 3/99. The position of objections raised by DACR/Intemal Audit Wing/ Controller General of Accounts Audit party against this Organisation has been exhibited in the Annexure.

Internal work study unit

(i) The Internal Work Study unit is common to the both the Departments, viz., Department of Legal Affairs and Legislative Department and other formations such as Income-tax Appellate Tribunal, Law Commission, Official Languages Wing, Central Agency Section and Vidhi Sahitya Prakashan.

(ii) In addition to the normal O&M activities during the year, the unit has done the following work during 1997-98:

1. Work Measurement Study of O.L. and Hind Section of Legislative Department.
2. Work Measurement Study of recreation of Post of Librarian Grade I in Law Commission.
3. Issue of Revised Questionnaire for Annual O&M Inspection.
4. Issue of instructions in respect of Records Management and Preservation.
5. Introduction of Award Scheme for Central Government Employees as well as Members of General Public.
6. Introduction of Scheme for grant of Cash Awards to Sections for showing high performance in Q&M activities.
7. Review of 150 files and recording of 125 files in IWSU itself.

   (ii) Annual O&M Inspection for the year 1997-98 of 49 Sections of Department of Legal Affairs and Legislative Department have been initiated during the year 1998-99 (Reports in respect of I received till date).

The following Work Measurement studies are in hand:-

1. Admn. III.
2. NALSA.
3. Branch Secretariat, Mumbai.
4. Newly created Cell for monitoring the functions of Government Lawyers.
5. Computerisation of various functions of Department of Legal Affairs is in progress.

Progress in the use of hindi in official work in the departmentof legal affairs

(i) The Department of Legal Affairs has taken following steps to implement various instructions issued by the Department of Official Language on the progressive use of Hindi for official purposes of the Union as contained in the Official Languages Act, 1963 and the Official Languages (Use for Official Purposes of the Union) Rules, 1976:

(a) Creation of Hindi posts for Implementation of Official Language Policy: Following posts have been created in the Department for implementation of the Official Language Policy:

(1) Deputy Director (OL) 1 post

(2) Assistant Director (OL) 1 post

(3) Senior Hindi Translator 1 post

(4) Junior Hindi Translator 3 posts.

(b) Notification under Rule 10(4) of the Official Languages (Use for Official Purposes of the Union) Rules, 1976: Ibis Department was notified under Rule 10(4) of the Official Languages Rules, 1976 on 21.3.1980. Orders were issued on 25.7.1989 directing all officers and employees proficient in Hindi to submit drafts, etc., of all communications addressed to State Governments/Union territories and to private individuals and also to Central Government offices located in Regions 'A' and 'B' and of communications in reply to letters, etc., received in Hindi or signed in Hindi including appeals, representations, etc., from the employees only in Hindi. Instructions in this regard are reiterated every year for strict compliance.

(c) Organisation of Hindi Day/Hindi Month: With a view to accelerating the use of the Official Language and to increasing the awareness of the employees as regards the Official Language Policy and the various incentive

schemes for using Hindi in official work, 'Hindi Day' was celebrated in the Department on 14.9.1998. Hon'ble Minister of State for Law, Justice and Company Affairs and Law Secretary in their messages appealed to the officers and employees of the Department to adopt Hindi in their day-to-day official work. In order to make the various programmes organised in this connection effective, 'Hindi Month' was organised in the Department from 14.9.1998 to 13.10.1998. This was done with the twin objectives of (a) giving wider publicity to the various schemes, and (b) generating maximum output in terms of work done in Hindi. During the 'Hindi Month', "Hindi Essay Competition', "Hindi Typing Competition" and "Hindi Noting and Drafting Competition" were organised. 41 officers/employees of the Department participated in these competitions.

(d) Creation of check-points for implementation of orders relating to the Official Language: A review of the check-points for implementation of orders relating to the Official Language was made and orders for creation of adequate number of check-points (eight) in accordance with Rule 12 of the Official Languages Rules, 1976 were issued on 16,11.1994. The effectiveness of check-points is being regularly monitored through the quarterly progress reports received from sections/offices.

(ii) In Sections/Units where the staff are proficient in Hindi, the use of Hindi in their day-to-day work is being encouraged. Work relating to the grant of various types of leave is being done in Hindi. Almost all cases relating to House Building Advances, GPF Advances and withdrawals, etc., are also being processed in Hindi and orders are also being issued in Hindi.

(iii) All general orders, notifications, resolutions and administrative reports, etc., are invariably issued in bilingual form. All letters received in Hindi are invariably replied to in Hindi only. Strict vigilance is maintained to ensure that there is no violation of the relevant rules in this regard.

(iv) Specimens of standard drafts of letters sent frequently by various sections have been collected and these have been translated into Hindi. All the standard drafts have thus been prepared in Hindi and English so that the staff can make use of them without any difficulty. All forms of the Department have also been translated into Hindi. Entries in service books are also being made in Hindi. All rubber stamps, name plates, signboards, etc., are invariably prepared in bilingual form.

(v) Devnagari typewriters am available in adequate number in the Department. Efforts are, however, continuing to increase the number of Devnagari typewriters. All the 32 electronic typewriters in the Department are bilingual.

(vi) A time-bound programme for imparting Hindi/ Hindi Stenography/Hindi typing training has been prepared under which 5 employees are nominated for Hindi training, 4 LDCs are nominated for Hindi typing training and 5 stenographers are nominated for Hindi Stenography training every year. One employee of the Department has passed Pragaya examination with distinction and 1 stenographer has passed Hindi Stenography examination with distinction. One employee of the Branch Secretariat, Chennai has also passed Prabodh Hindi Examination with distinction. 37 employees of die Main Secretariat of the Department were also awarded Cash Awards for participation in various incentive schemes for promotion of Hindi.

(vii) Last meeting of the Hindi Advisory Committee of the Ministry was held under the Chairmanship of Hon'ble Minister on the 15th September, 1997. Decisions taken in the meeting are being implemented. Decisions taken in the Central Official Language Implementation Committee meeting held under the Chairmanship of Secretary, Department of Official Languages on 30th January, 1997 are also being implemented. A separate Official Language Implementation Committee for the Department of Legal Affairs has been constituted for more effective implementation of the Official Language Policy in the Department and its offices.

(viii) Presidential orders issued by the Department of Official Language on the recommendations contained in Parts 1, U, III, IV and V of the Report of the Committee of Parliament on Official Language are being implemented in the Department and its offices.

Official languages section

(1) The Official Language Section of the Department organised various schemes and competitions in every quarter from 1.1.1998 to 30.9.1998 to mark the Golden Jubilee of India's Independence. For the nothing and drafting scheme for Match, 1998 and competitions which were held in June, 1998, the prizes were given by the Secretary (LD) to the successful candidates on 10th July, 1998. For the noting and drafting schemes of 6/98 and 9/98 and translation, Hindi typing speed and essay competitions were orgainsed together for the Golden Jubilee of India's Independence on "Hindi Fortnight". A large number of officers and employees participated in the competitions. The cassette titled "Nayi Manzil Ki Nayi Rah" was shown during Hindi Fornight. "Hindi Diwas" was celebrated on 14th September, 1998. On this occasion, the message of Home Minister on the use of Hindi *in Official Work was read by Hon'ble Secretary (LD) in the presence of Officers and staff of the Department.

A Prize distribution function was held on 14-09-1998 for Hindi Fortnight as well as conclusion of Golden Jubilee celebration of India's Independence.

(2) The members of the staff who had no knowledge of Hindi were deputed for Hindi Training under the Hindi teaching scheme. Staff members who were eligible for Hindi typing and Hindi shorthand classes, were deputed in various batches for training.

(3) An Official Language implementation Committee under the Chairmanship of Joint Secretary and Legislative Counsel (Admn.) is functioning in the Department. The Committee meets regularly every quarter to review the implementation of the instructions regarding the use of Hindi in official work and the Hindi Teaching Scheme. On the occassion of the Golden Jubilee Celebrations of India's Independence, a special issue of this Department's house journal 'Vidhayi Patrika' called 'Swaranjayanti Visheshank was published. Its printed copies were received during this year and distributed among all Officers/Sections.

5

Indian Democracy and Government

India, a Union of States, as a Sovereign Socialist Secular Democratic Republic with a parliamentary system of government. The Republic is governed in terms of the Constitution, which was adopted by Const-ituent Assembly on 26 November, 1949 and came into force on 26 January, 1950.The Constitution which evisages parliamentary from of government is federal in structure with unitary features. President of India is constitutional head of executive of the Union. Article 74(1) of the Constitution provides that there shall be a Council of Ministers with the Prime Minister as head to aid and advise president who shall, in exercise of his functions, act in accordance with such advice. Real executive power thus vests in Council of Ministers with Prime minister as head. Council of Ministers is collectively responsible to the House of the People (Lok Sabha). Similarly, in states, Governor is head of executive, but it is the Council of Ministers with Chief Minister as head in whom real executive power vests. Council of Ministers of a state is collectively responsible to Legislative Assembly.

The Constitution distributes legislative power between Parliament and state legislatures and provides for vesting of residual powers in Parliament. Power to amend the Constitution also vests in Parliament.

The union and its territory

India comprises 25 states and seven union territories. States are: Andhra Pradesh, Assam, Arunachal Pradesh, Bihar, Goa, Gujraat, Haryana, himachal Pradesh, Jammu and Kashmir, Karnataka, Kerala, Madhya Pradesh, Maharashtra, Manipur, Megthalaya, Mizoram, Nagaland, Orissa, Punjab, Rajasthan, Sikkim, Tamil Nadu, Tripura, Uttar Pradesh and West Bengal. Union territories are: Andaman and Nicobar Islands, Chandigarh, Dadra and Nagar Haveli, Daman and Diu, Delhi, Lakshadweep and Pondicherry.

The Constitution of India provides for a single and uniform citizenship for whole of India. Every person who was at commencement of the Constitution (26 January 1950) domiciled in the territory of India and: (a) who was born in the territory of India or (b) either of whose parents was born in the territory of India or (c) who has been ordinarily resident in the territory of India for not less than five years immediately preceding such commencement, shall be a citizen of India. The Citizenship Act, 1955 provides for acquisition and termination of citizenship after the commencement of the Constitution.

The Constitution offers all citizens, individually and collectively, some basic freedoms. These are guaranteed in the Constitution in the form of six broad categories of Fundamental Rights which are justiceable. Article 12 to 35 contained in Part III of the Constitution deal with Fundamental Rights. These are: (i) right to equality including equality before law, prohibition of discrimination on grounds of religion, race, caste, sex or place of birth and equality of opportunity in matters of employment; (ii) right to freedom of speech and expression; assembly; association or union; movement; residence; and right to practice any profession or occupation (some of these rights are subject to security of the State, friendly relations with foreign countries, public order, decency or morality); (iii) right against exploitation, prohibiting all forms of forced labour, child labour and traffic in human beings; (iv) right to freedom of conscience and free profession, practice and propagation of religion; (v) right of any section of citizens to conserve their culture, language or script and right of minorities to establish and administer educational institutions of their choice, and (vi) right to constitutional remedies for enforcement of Fundamental Rights.

By the 42nd Amendment of the Constitution, adopted in 1976, Fundamental Duties of the citizens have also been enumerated. Article 51 'A' contained in Part IV A of the Constitution deals with Fundamental Duties. These enjoin upon a citizen among other things, to abide by the Constitution, to cherish and follow noble ideals which inspired our national struggle for freedom, to defend the country and render national service when called upon to do so and to promote harmony and spirit of common brotherhood amongst all people of India transcending religious, linguistic and regional or sectional diversities.

The Constitution lays down certain Directive Principles of State Policy which though not justiceable, are 'fundamental in governance of the country' and it is 'the duty of the State to apply these principles in making laws'. These lay down that the State shall strive to promote welfare of people by securing and protecting as effectively as it may a social order in which justice–social, economic and political, shall inform all institutions of national life. The State shall direct its policy in such a manner as to secure the right of all men and women to an adequate means of livelihood, equal pay for equal work and within limits of its economic capacity and development, to make effective provision for securing the right to work, education and to public assistance in the event of unemployment, old age, sickness and disablement or other cases of undeserved want. The State shall also endeavour to secure to workers a living wage, humane conditions of work, a decent standard of life and full involvement of workers in management of industries.

In economic sphere, the State is to direct its policy in such a manner as to secure distribution of ownership and control of material resources of community to subserve the common good and to ensure that operation of economic system does not result in concentration of wealth and means of production to common detriment.

Some of the other important directives relate to provisions of opportunities and facilities for children to develop in a healthy manner, free and compulsory education for all children up to the age of 14; promotion of educational and economic interests of scheduled castes, scheduled tribes and other weaker sections; organisation of village panchayats; separation of judiciary from executive, promulgation of a uniform civil code for whole country; protection of national monuments; promotion of justice on a basis of equal opportunity; provision of free legal aid; protection and improvement of environment and safeguarding of forests and wildlife of the country and promotion of international peace and security, just and honourable relations between nations, respect for international law, treaty obligations and settlement of international disputes by arbitration.

The Indian Constitution is a remarkable document as it strikes a balance between tradition and modernity, between a federal structure and a strong centre and between the demands of social justice and the rights of the individual. However, as we enter the 50th year of our Independence, perhaps it would be desirable to take a close second look at the Constitution with a view to removing possible distortions and streamlining its functioning, feel the author.

Democracy is often described as government of the people, by the people and for the people. The Constitution, written as in the United States and other countries or unwritten but dependent on tradition as in the United Kingdom, lays down the framework for this form of government. But written or unwritten, there is a remarkable similarity between the two. In the United Kingdom the centre of power shifted first from the Crown to the nobles and then to the House of Commons. In the United States, judicial pronouncements have changed the complexion of the government. The federal Government has far more powers than was envisaged at first. All this was achieved by a process of evolution either by consensus as in the U.K. or by judicial pronouncements as it came up and a solution was found.

India became independent on August 15, 1947 and the Founding Fathers worked post haste to give the nation a new Constitution. The constitution was adopted by the Constitutent Assembly on November 26, 1949 and came into force on January 26, 1950. It was a remarkable achievement because many countries which became independent along with India were still floundering and trying to find their way in framing the Constitution. Countries, which became independent later, were looking at India's efforts. The Indian Constitution is a remarkable document as it strikes a balance between tradition and modernity, between a federal structure and strong centre between the demands of social justice and the rights of the individual and between conflicting demands in other areas.

Though the Founding Fathers were proud of the Constitution they had framed. they were also aware of their own limitations. As people move into a new house, they notice defects which had escaped the architect. Also conditions change and needs grow. Similarly, defects come to light as a Constitution comes into operation. Changes therefore become necessary and have to be made quickly and easily. As Dr. B.R. Ambedkar, the Law Minister, said on the day the Constitution was adopted, "The Assembly has not only refrained from putting a seal of finality and infallibility upon the Constitution by denying the people the right to amend the Constitution or making the amendment of the Constitution subject to the fulfilment of extraordinary terms and conditions, as in America or in Australia but has provided a more facile procedure foramending the Constitution". The President of the Constituent Assembly Dr. Rajendra Prasad observed "another important feature of the Constitution is that it enables amendments to be made without much difficulty".

Prime Minister Jawaharlal Nehru was even more forthright. Speaking on the first amendment made in 1951 he said, "People must realise that this great Constitution of ours, which we laboured for so long, is not a final or rigid thing which must either be accepted or broken. A Constitution which is responsive to their ideas, in that it can be revised here and there, they will respect it all the more and they will not fight against it. Otherwise if you make them feel that it is unchangeable and cannot be touched the only thing that can be done by people who wish to change it, is to try and break it. That is a dangerous thing and a bad thing. Therefore it is a desirable and a good thing for people to realise that this very fine Constitution which we have fashioned is good in so far as it goes but as society changes, as conditions change, we mend it in the proper way".

The members of the Constituent Assembly were conscious that they had been elected by members ofthe

Provincial Assemblies who had themselves been elected on a limited franchise. How could they put restrictions on the House of the People which was to be set up on the principle of universal adult franchise ? The leaders were also aware that in the years to come, conditions would change, new demands would be made and met and it would be the duty of the new rulers to meet the challenges as they came up. It was therefore that they left the way open for easy amendments without going through the arduous process of forming a new Constituent Assembly.

Events proved that the Founding Fathers of the Constitution showed robust common sense when they decided that the process of amending the Constitution should be easy. The first amendment was made in 1951 to make it possible among other things to carry out land reforms and abolish the zamindaris. Also, it was decided that reasonable restrictions could be placed on the exercise of Fundamental Rights in the interests of society. Since then, the Constitution has been amended more than 75 times. Most of these amendments were made to remove difficulties in the working of the Constitution, but others like the one about Panchayati Raj and Municipalities gave an entirely new dimension to administration by devolution of powers to local self-government bodies. The amendment about reservation for women in legislative bodies will add one more dimension to the Constitution.

The result is that the Constitution today resembles an ancient edifice to which additions and modifications have been made from time to time to suit the needs but in the process, the character of the original structure has been changed beyond recognition. Some of the provisions of the Constitution like introducing prohibition or banning cow slaughter have been found to be impossible to implement. Others like drafting a Common Civil Code have met with stiff opposition form sections of society. Similarly many of the Directive Principles of State Policy have been reduced to mere expression of pious intentions.

The Constituent Assembly utilised the period between August 15, 1947 and November 26, 1949 to draft the Constitution which came into force on January 26, 1950. On August 15 1997 India completes fifty years of Independence. It will be in the fitness of things if the task of taking a second look at the Constitution is attempted so as to remove the cobwebs and to streamline the working. A Committee of Parliament can undertake the job with inputs from politicians, experts in constitutional law, academics and journalists. The changes can be made by the time the nation celebrates the 50th anniversary of the enforcement of the Constitution and the establishment of the Indian Republic.

The paths to peace and freedom and equal rights were strewn with throrns and hurdles were placed at all steps. The White rule became a blot on the world conscience. Denial to right to live brought an upsurge among the Black South Africans. In their struggle, they found India and the Indians settled there as a great sorce of inspiration. It was not because Mahatma Gandhi's association with South Africa in the initial years of his political life that made India so receptive to the aspirations of the Black South Africans.

Perhaps in the South African freedom movement and struglle for equality was seen the same psyche of the Indian people who suffered humiliation, imprisonment and torture in India during the ong independence struggle. Indians felt genuinely for the Black South Africans. So did the government.

In less than a decade's existence as an independent nation, India brought before the world a new concept of governance based on the principle of "Panchsheel". It was but natural for a country that has a long tradition of tolerance. India with numerous languages and multiplicity of religion itself symbolises co-existence. Mutual respect for each other, irrespective of differences, demonstrates Indian ethos.

It is in this context, the Bandung conference in April 1955 that adopted "Panchsheel" created a new concept for the world already handed over to violence and turmoil. The Bandung conference had five proponents: India, Indonasia, Burma, Sri Lanka and Pakistan. The Bandung conference was preceded by the bombing ofthe Air India plane carrying delegates and journalists over South China sea. Evidently, forces that wanted the settlement of disputes through terrorism asserted their right to show their way of solving issue and problems.

India as a peace loving nation made its mark as a peacekeeper under the leadership of the United Nations. Peacekeeper's role came to India primarily because of its sense of fairness, coupled with the Indian armed forces' record of efficient functioning in warlike situationss. More than that, Nehru's approach usually proceeded on the assumption that peace cannot be promoted by creating positons of strength. On the contrary, the creation of positions of strength might become a threat to peace for every party will try to increase naturally its strength vis-s-vis its competitors for power, and such an attempt is bound to be counter productive, apart from being suicidal. It was Nehru's considered view that a deliberate policy of friendship with other countries goes further in gaining security than almost anything else. But in his Lifetime China proved it wrong when it attacked India in 1962.

India was involved in the Korean crisis within a few months of gaining Independence. After the Korean issue was brought before the Unied Nations in 1947, K.P.S. Menon was designated as the chairman of the first United Nations Temporary Commission on Korea. Ever since India was connected with the deliberations concerning the Korean peninsula, gearing its efforts towards reuniting the two halves of the nation. Unfortunately, even after 50 years the situation in Korea remains the same as before. It became a victim of cold war situation with foreign forces still operating on the South Korean soil.

In 1948, India once again headed the second United Nations Commission on Korea in June 1950, India's involvement was not confined only to the four corners ofthe U.N. Subsequently, India wa selected to be the chairman of the Neutral Nations Repatriation Commission that supervised the return of the prisoners of war to their respective countries. India devised a formula to solve the repatriation problem.

India's resolution at the General Assembly in the United nations formed the basis of the Armistice Agreement on December 3, 1952. When cease-fire was effected in Korea, the Custodian Force of India (CFI) took over the work of repatriation of POWs. In his report, Major General S.P.P. Throat has said force was not used for the purpose of taking out prisoners of war for explanations, while the CFI found that more than 90 per cent of the prisoners were anti-communist. Only 4 per cent of POWs were procommunist.

Over the past 35 years, India was called upon by the United Nations on many occasions to undertake peacekeeping work in various parts of the world. The most important among them may be mentioned as India's peacekeeping role in Gaza after the Arab-Israel war in 1967 and in the Congo operations. Between 1948 and June 30, 1994, over 650,000 military personnel have served in the UN peacekeeping force. Form the average of 300 million dollars expenditure on peacekeeping, it went up to 640 million in 1989. In 1994, the budget peaked to 3.8 billion dollars.

Indian forces found their active role in restoring peace in Cambodia, Mozambique and Somalia. In all these operations, Indian forces acquitted themselves creditably.

There is no doubt that India will continue to play an important role in the Un peacekeeping in the future. For an enhanced and effective role, India needs to set up a necessaty organisation which could be set in motion quickly. Given the emerging world order, instability and conflict will be a recurring phenomenon inthe decades to come.

Politicians will try to shy away from the task on the ground that it will mean opening a Pandora's box, which it will certainly be. The States will demand more powers even autonomy, while some will ask for more powers for the centre. Conflicting claims and demands will be made. Should we have directive Principles of State Policy which cannot be enforced in a Court of Law? All these and more will have to be looked into.

But there are some problems which cannot be pushed under the carpet any more. When the Constitution was framed, the Assembly had to a large extent placed before itself the Westminster form of Government. In such a form of government, two political parties vie for power. There is a general agreement on basic problems and policies. The Founding Fathers had possibly hoped that in course of time in India also, two rival parties would emerge. But this has not happened. We have a plethora of political parties. Three successive elections to the Lok Sabha did not give any political party a clear majority. Even when a politial party has the majority, its leader is always worried about keeping his flock together. Policies are often framed not so much for national good but for narrow political ends.

But what is the remedy if the electorate does not give a clear verdict in election after electon? The Constitution has no provision for direct rule by the President at the Centre because this might result insubversion of democracy and the establishment of a dictatorship. At the State level, the Constitution provides for imposition of President's rule. Dr. Ambedkar had expressed the hope that his provision might never be used. Events have proved otherwise and in the last 47 years, it has been used more than 100 times. There is justification for doing so when separatist forces and militancy pose threat to democracy as in Punjab, Jammu & Kashmir and Assam but no justificaton when it is used for political purposes.

But what is the way out at the Centre or in the States if no party gets a clear majority in election after election? A poor country can ill afford the luxury of election after election without a verdict in favour of any single party. Students and scholars of political science and leaders of political parties have been worried about this for a long time. Even during the days of Mrs. Indira Gandhi a suggestion was made that India should go in for a presidential form of government. The former Union Minister and senior parliamentarian Mr. Vasant Sathe has long been advocating this and has also said that this change can be made with a few changes in the Constitution.

There is another area where the distortion is worsening every day. Under the original scheme of things, a population of 7½ lakh elected a member of the Lok Sabha. The first Lok Sabha thus had 489 elected members. The Constitution also provided that the number of seats would go up according to the figures of population in the previous census. The seats went up to 545 by 1976. But it was felt that the increase gave an unfair advantage to the States which did not take up the family planning programme in earnest. Therefore, the number of seats in the Lok Sabha and in the Assemblies was frozen at the figures of 1976. By an amendment of the Constitution it was decided that the readjustment ofseats on the basis of population would be made only after the figures of the first census after the year 2000 were publidhed. The next Lok Sabha election would be held in 2001 which is also the year in which the next census will be held. By then the figures of the census are not likely to be available. But a serious thought will have to be given now to the question of the ratio between the population and the number of seats in the Lok Sabha and the State Assemblies. If the original scheme of one Lok Sabha member for every 7.50 lakh population were to be followed the Lok Sabha todays should have a membership of more than 1300. By the turn of the century the population of India is likely to go up to 100 crore and the membership of the Lok Sabha would have to be more than 1400. The Uttar pradesh Assembly would similiarly have a strength of 800 today. It will be impossible to manage such a large House.

But then if this is not done, the Lok Sabha constituencies would be so large in terms of population that it will be impossible for a candidate to contact the voters and for a candidate to contact the voters and for the M.P. to maintain contacts with his constituency. Outer Delhi today has electorate of nearly 30 lakh. Thane in Maharashtra comes a close second with an electorate of 26 lakh. It is well nigh impossible for anyone to claim that he can look after the interests of such a large electorate much less to visit the distant areas regularly. Many constituencies of the U.P. Assembly today have the same electorate as the Lok Sabha had in 1952. A fresh delimitation can only solve the problem partially. What is needed is a fresh look and a new initiative.

Under the present system the candidate who gets the largest number of votes is declared elected. Frequently the combined votes of the other candidates are more than his votes. It has also happened that a political party might get a majority of the seats. A swing of a mere 5 per cent can make a tremendous difference. Any review of the Constitution must look at this anomaly and find ways to remove it.

The Union executive consists of President, Vice President and Council of Ministers with Prime Minister at the head to aid and advice President.

President is elected by members of an electoral college consisting of elected members of both House of Parliament and Legislative Assumblies of the states in accordance with the system of proportional representation by means of single transferable vote. To secure uniformity among states *inter se* as well as parity between the states, as a whole, and the Union, suitable weightage is given to each vote. President must be a citizen of India, not less than 35 years of age and qualified for election as member of the Lok Sabha. His term of office is five years and he is eligible for re-election. His removal from office is to be in accordance with procedure prescribed in Article 61 of the Constitution. (He may, by writing under his hand addressed to Vice President, resign his office.)

Executive power of the Union is vested in President and is exercised by him either directly or through officers subordinate to him in accordance with the Constitution. Supreme Command of defence forces of the Union also vests in him.

President summons, prorogues, addresses, sends messages to Parliament and dissolves the Lok Sabha; promulgates Ordinances at any time, except when both Houses of Parliament are in session; makes recommendations for introducing financial and money bills and gives assent to bills; grants pardons, reprieves, respites or remissions of punishment or suspends, remits or commutes sentences in certain cases. When there is a failure of the constitutional machinery in a state, he can assume to hmself all or any of the functions of the government of that state. President can proclaim emergency in the country if he is satisfied that a grave emergency exists whereby security of India or any part of its territory is threatened whether by war or external aggression or armed rebellion.

Vice president

Vice President is elected by members of an electoral college consisting of members of both Houses of Parliament in accordance with the system of proportional representation by means of single transferable vote. He must be a citizen of India, not less than 35 years of age and eligible for election as a member of the Rajya Sabha. His term of office is five years and he is eligible for re-election. His removal from office is to be in accordance with procudure prescribed in Article 67 b.

Vice Presidents is *ex-offico* Chairman of the Rajya Sabha and acts as President when the latter is unable to discharge his functions due to absence, illness or any other cause or till the election of a new President (to be held within six months) when a vacancy is caused by death, resignation or removal or otherwise of President. While so acting, he ceases to perform the function of the Chairman of the Rajya Sabha.

There is a Council of Ministers headed by PrimeMinister to aid and advise President in exercise of his functions. Prime Minister is appointed by President who also appoints other ministers on the advice of Prime Minister. The Council is collectively responsible to the Lok Sabha. It is the duty of the Prime Minister to communicate to President all decisions of Council of Ministers relating to administeration of affairs of the Union and proposals for legislation and information relating to them.

The Council of Ministers comprises Ministers who members of Cabinet, Ministers of State (independent charge), Ministers of State and Deputy Ministers.

Legislature of the Union which is called Parliament, consists of President and two Houses, known as Council of States (Rajya Sabha) and House of the People (Lok Sabha). Each House of Parliament has to meet within six months of its previous sitting. A joint sitting of two Houses can be held in certain cases.

A switch over to the Presidential Form of Government will be a far reaching change which can only be made after a nation wide debate. But the immediate problems of the electoral system need to be examined quickly. A 'hung' Lok Sabha or State Assembly leads to defections and politics of expendiency and negates democracy. We have to find an answer to it. Introduction of proportional representation is not prctical in a large country like India. But should we then have a system of direct election for half the seats and proportional representation for the other half? This experiment has been tried succesfully in Japan.

Another area for attention is the role of the Rajya Sabha and the Legislative Councils in some States. These were envisaged as chambers of revision but over the years have largely become chambers where the work is mostly duplicated. Our Rajya Sabha is neither as powerful as the Senate in the USA nor powerless as the

House of Lords in the U.K. Its powers and functioning deserve a close second look. Unlike the Lok Sabha, the Rajya Sabha is supposed to represent the States. It has therefore been laid down that its members should be normally resident in the State from which they are elected. But more and more instances come up where he does not live. It is easy to look at this as a technical violation of the Constitution. But another aspect is often overlooked. States like Punjab and Jammu & Kashmir were for long years been under President's rule and the Legislative Assemblies had been dissolved and could not elect members to the Rajya Sabha, elections to the Lok Sabha were also not held there. Should the people of these States be denied the right of representation at both the Central and State levels for no fault of their own? Election tot he Rajya Sabha from another state might not be strictly according to the letter of the Constitution but it at least gives a politician from such a State to put forward the views of the people and to air their grievances.

It is well known that militancy in Punjab was limited to a few districts and in Jammu & Kashmir to the Kashmir Valley. But since the Assembly had been dissolved and the State placed under Central rule, areas where there was comparative peace could also not go to the polls even for the Lok Sabha. They were penalised for no faults of theirs. Any review of the Constitution has to consider this question and find a solution.

It is to the credit of India that while other countries which became independent along with her have had long periods of dictatorship or military rule, democracy has continued to grow in India. The Indian voter has been no respecter of men and has not hesitated to throw out powerful leaders if he found that they were not performing well. The base has widened with the devolution of powers to the local self-governing bodies. The proposal to reserve seats for women in legislative bodies is proof of the fact that political parties forget their differences on giving greater powers to the neglected segments of society. Changes have been made in the Constitution to keep pace with the times.

As India enters the 50th year of her Independence it is time to do a soul searching and to examine whether the Constitution needs a close second look so as to remove the cobwebs and to remove the distortions and discrepancies.

If the Plan objectives and programmes are to be translated into reality, the close co-operation and co-ordination from the States is ess-ential. The economic reform programmes which form a guide-post of the Central direction could succeed only if the States are sincere and committed to the cause. Much of the benefits of direct investment depends on the policy and initiative of the State governments. Reforms can receive greater acceptability only if poverty alleviation measures are implemented vigorously, which has to be done by the States. The development of infrastructure and social sector has ultimately to be implemented by the States.

We have already noted that a vital constraint of growth and development is unchecked population. The family welfare programmes and population control mechanism are in the hands of State governments. Statistics show that some States have advanced in the direction while others are lagging behind. The story of success or failure in this direction has been caused by the extent to which the States are sincere and devoted to the cause. The newly revamped public distribution system of the deva Gowda government has decided to supply 10 kg of food grains at half the PDS price to 60 million families below the poverty line "in order that nobody could complain about the step as the aim was to benefit the poor." It may be recalled that during the Food

Ministers' conference at New Delhi in August 1996, the State Food Ministers refused to withdraw the PDS benefits from affluent classes and also to raise the price of ration items. Again, the identification of families below the poverty line lies with the State government. Though the Centre has asked the States to set up vigilance committees at the Panchayat level to supervise identification, the success of the scheme will largely depend on how sincere are the agencies entrusted with the responsibility, other things remaining the same.

In order to achieve the seven minimum basic services in particular and the rural development schemes in general, the Centre has instructed the States to constitute vigilance and monitoring committees at the block, district and State levels for the effective implementation of rural development programmes across the country. The government has taken action to strengthen the District Rural Development Agencies (DRDAs) with adequate technical staff at various levels. These are important agencies for poverty alleviation programmes. Thus, at every level of plan efforts, success will depend chiefly on the States' implementation level.

The Common Minimum Programme (CMP) provides a clear indication of the Government's commitment to accelerate the process of economic reforms and to address some areas of weakness that have emerged.

Among the major themes of the CMP are:

— An overarching commitment to growth with social justice.

— A growth target of 7 per cent year in the next 10 years.

— A commitment to fiscal prudence with the goal of reducing the fiscal deficit to below 4% of GDP.

— A commitment to strengthen anti-poverty programmes and target subsidies in favour of the poor.

— A commitment to increase investment in the social sectors.

— A commitment to continue the process of tax reform and bring about a phased reduction in customs duties.

— A commitment to decontroal and reform in the agricultural sector.

— A target of maintaining 12 per cent annual growth of industry.

— A target of $ 10 billion a year of foreign direct investment.

— A commitment to reform and restructuring public sector enterprises, including through disinvestment.

— A commitment to developing the infrastructure sectors through all modes of investment, public and private domestic and foreign.

The Government has moved swiftly to implement the agenda outlined in the CMP.

The programme of tax reform has been carried forward along the lines articulated by the Tax Reforms Commitee, import duties have been reduced for a wide range of products. The intension is to eventually move to duty rates comparable to those prevailing in other developing South-East Asian economies, the Modvat system of rebates of excise tax on imputs to the singly most important industrial sector in India, namely, textiles, has been extended, the surcharge on corporate taxation reduced by half and introduced Minimum Alternate Tax as a measure of broadening the base of taxation.

The Government is committed to fiscal prudence by reducing the fiscal deficit to 5 per cent of GDP for 1996-97 as compared to 5.9 per cent in 1995-96 (Revised Estimates). A number of initiatives to deal with three critical areas of weakness in the economy are: agriculture, infrastructure and social sectors.

In agriculture, the budget has made allocations for strengthening the capital base of the National Bank for Agricultural and Rural Development, the principal refinance institution in agricultural credit. It has also provided funds for re-capitalising Regional Rural Banks and has launched an important new initiative for private local area banks. Agricultural infrastructure will be strengthened through a large special allocation to finance completion of a number of irrigation schemes.

For infrastructure, a number of fiscal incentives are being provided in the budget. The tax holiday earlier provided for power, telecommunications and road transport has been extended to other infrastructure sectors such as water supply, sewerage and irrigation. It also exempts from income-tax the income of dedicated infrastructure funds which invest in equity and debt instruments of infrastructure companies. The existing income tax incentive available for long-term savings under Section 88 of the Income Tax Act has beden extened to include bonds issued by infrastructure companies or by financial institutions leading to infrastructure projects. The budget has also announced the formation of a new Infrastructure Development Finance Company (IDFC) which will fill some critical gaps in financing of commercially viable infrastructure projects. This institution could act as a direct lender, as a refinance institution, as a channel for multilateral funds and as a provider of various types of financial guarantees for infrastructure projects. The intention is that the IDFC will induce investors in India and abroad to make available long-term funds at the lowest market rates. The budget has alo provided resources for the National Highway Authority of India to help fund its operations.

In the social sectors, a number of schemes have been launched to strengthen the provision of basic minimum services and has generally expanded allocations for social services and anti-poverty programmes.

The Government welcomes foreign investment and has taken a number of concrete steps to achieve this objective. The Foreign Investment Promotion Board has been restructured to make the process of foreign investment approval speedier and more transparent. 350 foreign investment projects have been cleared involving a total foreign equity of US $ 4 billion. A new Foreign investment Promotion Council has been established aimed at reaching out to foreign investors and represent their concerns to the Government. The Government has announced that the list of 35 industries which are eligible for automatic approval of foreign investment upto 51 per cent of equity will be expanded in order to accelerate the approval process. The regulations governing foreign institutional investor have been amended to allow these investors to make equity investments in unlisted companies. Hitherto, they were limited to investing in listed companies only. The limit of investment of 5 per cent of total equity in a single company by an individual FII has been rasied to 10 per cent. The Securities and Exchange Board of India (SEBI) regulations are being amended to allow FIIs to set up 100 per cent debt funds to facilitate FII investment in corporate debt instruments. The guidelines for Euro issues have been liberalised to ease access of Indian companies to international capital markets.

In the area of capital markets, landmark legislation enabling the establishment of depositories for share trading has been passed during the Budget session of Parliament. The first depository is expected to become operational in November this year. Stronger guidelines have been issued for disclosure in the offer documents of primary issues and a number of other steps have been taken to strengthen investor protection. New guidelines have been brought out for mutual funds in general and for money market mutual funds in particular.

The process of financial sector reform has been continued on several fronts. Reserve requirements of banks have been reduced; many more public sector banks have reached capital adequacy norms set out several years ago; regulation of interest rates on bank deposits has been reduced so that they remain only on maturities upto one year; and more private sector banks have become operational. Interest rates charged on loans have been comletely deregulated for Regional Rural Banks to improve their financial viability. It has been decided to allow private sector local area banks to be set up which will operate in two or three districts. These banks will be subject to RBI regulations but will have lower initial capital requirements and will benefit from the interest rate deregulation extended to Regional Rural banks. The process of reforms in the banking sector has borne fruit in the form of significant reduction in non-performing asset of public sector banks and higher profits.

Non-Bank Financial Companies (NBFCs) which comply with the dual requirement of credit rating and prudential norms have been allowed freedom to fixed interest rates on deposits. At the same time, the reserve bank of India has imposed a ceiling on interest rates which can be offered by the mutual benefit financial companies (MBFCs) which do not meet the prudential standards set by RBI.

A number of steps have been taken to strengthen the market for Government securities including the issue of guidelines for primary dealers in Government securities. The first set of such dealers have begun operation. Following the announcement in the budget, legislation is being proposed to provide statutory backing to new, Insurance Regulatory Authority. Similarly, quick action has been taken to establish the Disinvestment Commission announced in the budget.

Public sector

Since Independence, the public sector in India has been guided by the Industrial Policy Resolution of 1956, which had as its objectives the acceleration of the rate of economic growth and speeding up of the industrialisation as means of achieving the socialistic pattern of society. Since in the initial phase of industrialisation, the capital was scare, the state sector assumed the predominance and direct responsibility for industrial development. The size of public sector in India is indeed very large. It includes government departments and its compaines whether in the Central or state sector, irrigation and power projects, railways, posts and telegraphs, ordnance factories and other departmental undertakings, banking, insurance, financial and other services. The focus here is however, on the Central public sector enterprises established as Government companies or statutory corporations excluding banking units.

After the initial exuberance of public sector entering into new areas of industrial manufacturing, providing technical services, trading, financial and services sectors, the public enterprises started facing various problems, some of these problems were due to historical reasons, while others were related to poor project management, over-manning, obsolete technology, poor order book positions etc. All these put together, the public sector as a whole started showing results far below the desired level in comparison to the investments made in them.

The Government announced a new Industrial Policy on 24 July 1991 which envisages liberalisation, competitive environment. The new Policy has laid down certain specific areas in respect of the public enterprises which are to be emphasized in order to make them better performers and more competitive. The slient features of the new Industrial Policy on the Public Sector are: (i) Portfolio of public sector investments will be reviewed with a veiw to focus the public sector on strategic, high-tech and essential infrastructure. Whereas some reservation for the public sector is being retained, there would be no bar for area exclusively to be opened up to the private sector selectively. Similarly, the public sector will also be allowed entry in areas not reserved for it; (ii) Public enterprises which are chronically sick and which are unlikely to be turned around will for the formulation of revival, rehabilitation schemes, be referred to the Board for Industrial and Financial Reconstruction (BIFR), or other similar high level institutions created for the purpose. A social security mechanism will be created to protect the interest of workers likely to be affected by such rehabilitation packages; (iii) in order to raise resources and encourage wider public participation, a part of the governement's share-holding in the public sector would be offered to mutual funds, financial institutions, general public and workers; (iv) Boards of public sector companies would be made more professional and given greater powers; (v) there will be a greater thrust on performance improvement through the Memoranda of Understanding (MOU) system through which management would be granted greater autonomy and will be held accountable. Technical expertise on the part of the Goernment would be upgraded to make the MOU negotiations and implementation more effective;

and (vi) to facilitate a fuller discussion on performance, the MOU singed between Government and the public enterprise would be placed in Parliament. While focussing on major management issues, this would also help place matters on day to day operations of public enterprises in their perspective.

As a major step for implementation of the Policy, the Government of India has disinvested varying percentage of its share-holdings in some PSUs. So far, the shares of 39 PSUs, have been disinvested in favour of the financial institutions, mutual funds, banks, foreign institutional investors and the public. This resulted in disinvestment of 152.07 crore share in 39 public sector undertakings and a sum of Rs. 9,794 crore was realised. The shares of these companies are now listed on the stock exchanges. The valuation of the equity of these enterprises on the stock exchanges reflects the preceptions of the public in general and investors in particular of the performance and the expectations of the public from these enterprises. Besides, the Government has also offered a part of its equity holdings in some of these enterprises in favour of the employees, in order to encourage the employees participation in the managements a sence of commitment and belonging to an enterprise.

Over a period of time, the public enterprises have been faced with the chronical sickness and mounting losses. In the case of some of the enterprises, which have incurred huge losses and had eroded their networth, in order to formulate the revival/rehabilitation packages, a number of these enterprises have been referred to the Board for Industrial and Financial Reconstruction (BIFR). So far, 54 sick enterprises have been referred to BIFR for revival/rehabilitation. BIFR makes an independent assessment of the viability or otherwise of a particular enterprise afte keeping in the view points of the owner

(Government), the employees, the financial institutions and the other concerned. Under the new Industrial Policy, greater thrust has been laid on the evaluation of the performance, through the system of MOUs which has also started yielding positive results in the form of better performance from the public enterprises.

There has been appreciable growth in the investments in the public sector over the years. In 1951, the investment in five Central Public Sector was Rs. 29 crore. This investment has gone up to Rs. 147,587 crore in 245 enterprises as on 31 March 1993 and at Rs. 164,332 crore in 246 enterprises in 1993-94. Thus, during 1993-94, the investment in public sector has increased by Rs. 16,745 crore registering an increase of 11.35 per cent. The overall financial performance of the manufacturing and service group enterprises for the last two years is satisfactory.

Corporate sector

First company legislation in India was an Act for registration of joint stock companies enacted in 1850. This was followed by the Companies Act, 1913. As a result of recommendations of a committee under the chairmanship of C.H. Bhabha to make suggestions for company law reform, the Companies Act, 1956 was enacted as a Central lefislation. Prior to enactment of this Act, administration of companies' legislation was the responsibility of the state governments.

The Companies Act, 1956 has been in force for the last 38 years and during this period it has been amended over 16 times. Amendments of 1969, 1974, 1977 and 1988 are of special importance. By the amendment Act of 1969, system of appointing managing agencies or secretaries or treasurers in companies was abolished. Under the 1974 amendment, powers of High Court relating to certain sections of the Companies Act were transferred to

Company Law Board. Scope of Section 43A was enlarged so as to treat large private limited companies as deemed public limited companies. A new Section 58A was inserted to regulate acceptance of deposits by companies. Section 108A to Section 108H were introduced to check take-over bids by large groups. The 1977 amendment inserted, inter alia Section 634A enabling Company Law Board to enforce its orders under Section 17, 18, 19, 79 141 and 186 of the Act as a decree of a court of law. The Companies Act, 1956 provides various powers to Central Government and Company Law Board, to monitor, regulate and control the affairs of companies. Salient features of the 1988 amendments are: (a) setting up of an independent Company Law Board to exercise such judicial and quasi-judicial functions as are presently being exercised either by Court or Central government and proposed to be transferred to that Board; (b) dispensing with Government approval for managerial appointments and remuneration, subject to fulfilment of certain statutory guidelines which are proposed to be incorporated in the Act itself; (c) delinking of rates of depreciation from rates specified under the Income Tax Act and laying down rates of depreciation in the Act itself to reflect true and fair view of the state of affairs of the company; (d) protecting the interest of investors by providing for intervention by Company Law Board against non-payment of public deposits and certain other matters, compulsory redemption of preference shares in certain cases, requiring companies to disclose reasons for refusal to register transfer of shares, protecting the rights of thee transfree pending mutation of his name in the register of members, and also compulsory lilsting of all public issues; (e) reducing unnecessary cost or burden by requiring companies to attach only an abridged version for disclosure of information relating to conservation of energy, technology absorption, foreign exchange earnings and outgo as well as particulars of employees having some minimum stake in the company and drawing remuneration in excess of that drawn by managerial personnel.

The number of joint stock companies, both Government and non-Government incorporated under the Companies Act, 1956 and at work in India as on 31 March 1994 was 3,08,324. Of these 3,05,625 were limited by shares, 349 with unlimited liability and 2,350 were limited by guarantee or were associations not for profit. The 3,05,625 companies limited by shares have paid up capital of Rs. 1,04,890.8 crore. These comprised 38,000 public limited companies and 2,67,625 private limited companies with paid up capital of Rs. 70,112.1 and Rs. 34,778.7 crore respectively.

During 1993-94, 30,393 companies were registered under the Companies Act. These include 18 Government companies and 30,273 non-government companies with liability limited by shares, 13 non-government companies with unlimited liability and 89 non-government companies with liability limited by guarantee and associations not for profit. Of the 30,291 companies limited by shares registered during the year, 3,625 were public limited companies with an aggregate authorised capital of Rs. 5,456.2 crore and 26,666 were private limited companies with an aggregate authorised capital of Rs. 3,152.1 crore.

Section 60 of the Companies Act requires that prospectuses issued by or on behalf of the companies or in relation to an intended company inviting offers from the public for the subscription or purchase of any shares or debentures be delivered to the Registrar of Companies for registration. Section 67(3) provides that if the offer or invitation can properly be regarded as not being calculated to result, directly or indirectly, in the shares or debentures becoming available for subscription or purchase by persons other than those receiving offer or inviation, as being of a domestic concern of the persons making or receivinng such offer or invitation, shall not be treated as made to the public. Thus, prospectuses for issue of shares or debentures by private placement are not required to be registered with the Registrar of Companies. During the year ending 31 March 1994, 525 non government, non-financial public limited companies delivered to the Registrar of Companies for registration, the copies of prospectuses under Section 60 of the Act raising an amount of Rs. 7,952.8 crore from public as against 426 prospectuses delivered by the companies in the previous year for raising an amount of Rs. 6,331.1 crore. Of the 525 companies which issued prospectuses during 1993-94, 494 companies (or 94 per cent) invited applications for equity share capital, of the remaining 31 companies, invited applications for equity shares as well as debentures and 27 for debentures only.

Of the total amount of Rs. 7,952.8 crore issued through prospectuses during 1993-94, Rs. 3,542.7 crore (44.5 per cent approximately) was in respect of equity shares, Rs. 4,386.1 crore (55.1 per cent approximately) for debentures and balance of Rs. 24 crore (0.3 per cent) in respect of preference shares capital amounting to Rs. 4,310.7 crore or 54.2 per cent of the total amount covered by the prsopectuses, was offered to the public and balance of Rs. 3,642.1 crore or 45.8 per cent was earmarked for firm allotment to the promoters, directors, existing shareholders and employees of the companies, non-resident Indians, financial institutions, banks and the state industrial development corporations.

During 1993-94, 259 companies went into liquidation or otherwise became defunct or ceased to work and were struck off under Section 560 (5) of the Companies Act, 1956.

The following five committees of the National Development Council were constituted to go into some of the critical areas of development: (i) Committee on Austerity, (ii) Committee on Population, (iii) Committee on Employment, (iv) Committee on Micro-Level Planning; and (v) Committee on Literacy.

The meeting of the National Development Council held on 5 April 1993 considered the report of the NDC Committee on Austerity. The Council generally endorsed the recommendations of the report of the Committee. It was also decided to set up a NDC Committee on Power. Accordingly, NDC Committee on Power under the Chairmanship of Chief Minister, Maharashtra, was constituted to examine measures to make state electricity boards economically viable by recasting tariffs, improving efficiency and considering delinking of distribution from generation.

A Committee headed by Deputy Chairman, Planning Commission was constituted to evolve a suitable formula for distribution of Central assistance to Non-special Category States. The suggestions made by the Committee were discussed by the NDC in its meeting on 23-24 December 1991, wherein a consensus emerged and a revised formula evolved which was made the basis for allocation of Central Plan assistance to the states for the Eighth Plan. Under the criterion of the progress in respect of national objectives, the approved formula highlights four objectives, viz., (a) population control and maternal and child health; (b) universalisation of primary education; (c) on-time completion of externally aided projects; and (d) land reforms.

During the 43 year period (1950-51 to 1993-94), Net National Product (NNP) at factor cost at 1980-81 prices increased from 40,454 crore to Rs. 2,02,670 crore implying compound growth rate of 3.8 per cent per annum.

Advance estimates of GDP for 1994-95 project a growth rate of 5.3 per cent over 1993-94.

During the First Five year Plan (1951-56), national income increased by 3.6 per annum. In the Second Five Year Plan (1956-61), however, the growth rate actually achieved was four per cent annum against the target of 4.5 per cent per annum.

In the Third Plan (1961-66), there was a sharp decline in the growth rate at 2.3 per cent per annum and fell well short of the target at 5.6 per cent per annum. This was primarily due to the steep fall in agricultural production and consequent decline in NNP at factor cost of 4.65 per cent in the last year of the Third Plan. However, during the subsequent three Annual Plans, the economy picked up and the growth rate during 1965-69 was 3.7 per cent per annum. Fourth Five year Plan (1969-74), the growth rate target was fixed at 5.7 per cent in terms of NDP at factor cost. However, the actual growth rate achieved was only 3.3 per cent per annum.

The economy took an up-turn during the Fifth Five Year Plan (1974-79). The growth rate fixed in terms of GDP at factor cost of 4.4 per cent per annum was over-achieved at 4.8 per cent annum for the Fifth Five Year Plan. In 1979-80, however, the economy faced a severe drought resulting in the decline of GDP at factor cost by 5.2 per cent over the previous year. The economy bounced back on the track during the Sixth Plan (1980-85) period when the rate of growth in GDP at factor cost at 5.6 per cent per annum surpassed the target of 5.2 per cent per annum. Despite successive drought condistions during the first three years of the Seventh Plan (1985-90), the economy has fared exceptionally well. The growth rate achieved during Deventh Plan period was six per cent per annum and this surpassed the target of five per cent per annum in GDP at factor cost for the Seventh Plan.

During 1991-92, the country faced a severe fiscal crisis and the balance of payment situation became so critical that exceptional measures had to be restored to. While the growth momentum enabled an increase in GDP by 5.4 per cent in 1990-91, the growth in 1991-92 was only 0.9 per cent. In 1992-93 the economy registered the growth of 4.3 per cent and this had been mainly due to high growth in agriculture and improvement in sectors of trade, hotel and restaurants, transport by other means, storage, communication and the public administration and defence, despite railways and banking and insurance sectors registering a decelerated growth. The GDP from agriculture and allied sectors recorded a growth of 5.1 per cent in 1992-93 as compared to 2.3 per cent in 1991-92.

Important policy reforms had been made during June 1991 towards liberalisation and structural adjustment of the economy. These measures have started showing results. The annual rate of inflation as measured by the wholesale price index declined from 13.6 per cent at the end of 1991-92 to seven per cent in 1992-93. The inflation rate stood at 10.8 per cent in 1993-94. The Eighth Plan has targeted for a GDP growth of 5.6 per cent per year, a substantial reduction in the average annual inflation rate, about five per cent and the average current account deficit of about 1.6 per cent of GDP.

Index of agricultural production with the triennium ending 1969-70 as base, rose from 71.9 at the end of First Plan to 86.7 at the end of Second Plan. During Third Plan performance of agriculture was not quite satisfactory. Widespread drought during 1965-67 slowed down the rate of growth in agricultural production and led to increased import of foodgrains and other items. Index of agricultural production reached the level of 80.8 in 1965-66 and 80.7 in 1966-67. These drought years also witnessed introduction of the best available agricultural technology for the first time in India in the form of high yield variety programme and multiple cropping programme. The folloeing years recorded substantial improvement in agricultural production. As a result, the index, after recovering to 98.9 points in 1967-68 increased steadily to 112.4 in 1973-74. The next year 1974-75 again a bad year for agriculture when the index declined to 108.6. This was followed by considerable improvement in 1975-76 when it touched 125.1. In 1976-77, the index registered a decline of 8.8 points and stood at 116.3 but again shot up to 132.9 in 1977-78 and 138 in 1978-79. The year 1979-80 witnessed a fall by 21 points when index number of agricultural production slipped to 117. It recovered to 135.3 in 1980-81.

The index number of agriculture production steadily rose to 158.4 in 1985-86. There was decline during 1986-87 to 152.5 and 151.3 in 1987-88. Thereafter it picked up steadily to 192 in 1990-91 and came down to 188.5 in 1991-92 and recovered to 195.8 in 1992-93. According to the revised triennium ending 1981-82 as base, the index numbers of agriculture production which stood at 85.9 in 1970-71 rose to 154.8 in 1993-94. During 1982-83 Kharif production was adversely affected due to wayward monsoon which was inadequate, uneven and untimely. Even so, fall in foodgrains production was only marginal, indicated by a drop of 5.4 points in the production index. Agricultural production registered significant improvement in 1983-84 which was near normal year from the point of view of weather conditions. Index of agricultural production increased from 137.5 in 1982-83 to 156.4 in 1983-84 and production of foodgrains touched a record level of 15,237 crore tonnes. Weather conditions during 1984-85 were not very satisfactory. As a result, production of foodgrains declined to 14,554 crore tonnes and index number of agricultural production also declined marginally to 154.6. During Kharif 1985, onset of the south-west monsoon was delayed over central and northern states and its behaviour during the season was erratic over many states. However, weather conditions during the rabi season were on the whole rather favourable to crop production. Consequently, foodgrains output during 1985-86 stood at 15.044 crore tonnes. Weather conditions during 1986-87 continued to be unsatisfactory. Monsoon was delayed over eastern states, while southern states experienced dry spells leading to moisture stress conditions. As a result only 14.342 crore tonnes of foodgrains production could be achieved during 1986-87. The year 1987-88 witnessed severe drought conditions in most parts of the country and the incidence of heavy floods in the eastern states. The foodgrains production consequently further fell down to 14.035 crore tonnes. During 1988-89 production of foodgrains recorded a new peak of 16,982 crore tonnes indicating a substaintial increase of 1.775 crore tonnes over the previous peak of 15.237 crore tonnes achieved in 1983-84. With the rainfall and weather situation being favourable during south-west monsoon 1989, the total foodgrains production reached another record level of 17.065 crore tonnes.

On account of erratic behaviour of south-west monsoon, foodgrains production in 1991-92 fell by 4.6 per cent to 16.337 crore tonnes from a record level of 17.64 crore tonnes in 1990-91. Production of rice and wheat was 7.467 crore tonnes and 5.676 crore tonnes respectively. There was a substantial decline in the production of coarse cereals and pulses. Production of oilseeds in 1991-92 was less than previous year's production of 18.60 crore tonnes. Production of foodgrains during 1992-93 was 17.948 crore tonnes and the production was recorded at 18.212 crore tonnes in 1993-94. Production of foodgrains during 1994-95 is expected to be of the order of 18.636 crore tonnes.

Production of oilseeds is expected to be around 2.251 crore tonnes. The thrust has been given for the growth and diversification of agriculture to achieve self-sufficiency in food and generate surpluses for exports during the Eighth Five year Plan Period (1992-97).

On the irrigation side the potential created on major, medium and minor schemes increased from 22.6 million ha in 1950-51 to 26.25 million ha at the end of the First Plan, 29.08 million ha by Second Plan, 33.57 million ha at the end of Third Plan 37.1 million ha by 1966-69. At the end of 1969-74 the potential created was 44.10 ha. By 1979-80, it touched 56.61 million ha and by 1984-85, it reached 65.22 million ha. Potential created by 1989-90 was 76.52 million ha by 1991-92, 81.09 million ha and by 1992-93 achievement was 83.01 million ha. The anticipated achievement by 1993-94 is 85.05 million ha. The target for 1994-95 isto create additional irrigation potential of 2.62 million hectare.

Under power sector, total installed capacity (including non-utility), which was only 2301 mw in 1950, increased to 78,367 mw by the end of March 1992. Against the capacity addition of 30,538.7 mw in public utilities envisaged during the Eighth Plan period (1992-97), the actual addition during the first three years (1992-95) were 12,674 mw.

Under the rural electrification programme, 4.70 lakh villages had been electrified out of 5.79 lakh villages (as per 1981 Census) by the end of the Seventh Plan, achieving 81.3 per cent level of electrification. Upto December 1994, 4.94 lakh villages were electrified.

Universal elementary education, eradication of illiteracy in the age group of 15-35 and development of vocational education to act as viable alternate stream have been the focal points of all programmes in the education sector during the Eighth Plan. Major initiatives in the form of Operation Black-board, non-formal education programme, Teacher Education, and District Primary Education Programme have been undertaken to achieve the goal of 'Education for All'. As on September 1993, 108.20 million children have been enrolled in primary schools and 39.91 million in upper primary schools. The Eighth Plan during its first three years could achieve an additional enrolment of 11.69 million in the primary schools and 7.06 million in upper primary sections making a total enrolment of 18.7 million during the Eighth Plan.

The emphasis of adult literacy programme has been on sustainability of literacy skills and the achievement of goals of rmediation, continuation and application of skills of actual living conditions. Total Literacy Campaign (TLC) and Post Literacy and continuing education programmes are designed to cater to the above objectives. The Eighth Plan target was to cover 100 million adult illiterates by 1991. About 41 million people have been made literate so far under various programmes.

Under Vocational Education, the Eighth Plan target is to divert about 11.63 lakh higher secondary students to the vocational stream. Upto the end of 1993-94, 9.12 lakh students were enrolled in 16,450 vocational sections approved in 570 schools. In order to boost the programme and activities in Vocational Education, Pt. Sunder Lal Sharma Central Institute of Vocational Education (PSSCIVE) has been established under NCERT at Bhopal on 1 July 1993.

In the higher education sector as on 1994, there are 153 universities, 34 demand universities, 7,958 colleges and total enrolment in the higher education system is about 48 lakh. In addition, there ia a vast network for technical education, including colleges and institutions offering courses in engineering, medical science, management, etc. In the technical education sector new initiatives like Technology Development Missions, establishemnt off corpus fund in the case of IITs, IIMs and IISc, Banglaore have been taken up recently.

Large investments in the industrial and mineral sector particularly from the beginning of the Second Plan have brought about a significant transformation in the industrial scene. This rate of industrial growth has not been uniform during this period. After a steady growth of about eight per cent during the initial period of 14 years, there was fluctuating trend in the industrial growth rate approaching near stagnancy in 1960-68, going upto a level of 9.6 per cent in 1976-77 and dropping to -1.6 per cent in 1979-80. During the last decade (1970-71 to 1979-80) the average growth rate has been about four per cent per annum. The average growth rate of industry in the Sixth Plan period (1980-85) amounts to nearly six per cent which is a small improvement over the average of about 5.3 per cent in the preceding five years.

Seventh Plan envisaged an average annual growth rate of 8.7 per cent in the output of industry sector. In the first year of the Seventh Plan i.e. 1985-86, the actual growth rate achieved was 8.7 per cent as per revised Index of Industrial Production (IIP) (Base 1980-81=100). In 1986-87, second year of the Seventh Plan, growth rate achieved was 9.2 per cent. However in 1987-88, the growth rate declined to 7.3 per cent due to decline in production towards the end of the year following unprecedented drought. In 1988-89, there was agian a recovery in the growth rate and the IIP recorded an increase to 8.7 per cent. In the last year of the Seventh Plan, there was slight deceleration in the growth rate, which was only 8.6 per cent due to sharp decline in growth rates of mining and electricity sectors. During

1990-91, the growth rate was 8.3 per cent and during 1991-92, the growth rate was 0.6 for industrial production. The industrial production registered an increase of 2.3 per cent in 1992-93 and 4.1 per cent in 1993-94.

Government initiated a number of measures late in Sixth Plan and in early years of Seventh Plan with the objective of removing constraints on industrial growth and providing a more liberal and congenial environment for development of industries. A number of steps were taken to liberalise industrial procedures relating to creation of capacity, imports of technology, etc., to encourage competition in Indian industry so as to ensure reasonable prices and improvement in quality. These include re-endorsement of capacities, delicensing of industries including specified MRTP and FERA industries and broad-banding of a large number of industries especially in areas of high technology industries linked with energy production and utilisation, as well as mass consumer goods industries. Provisions of the MRTP Act and FERA regulations were rationalised to facilitate entry into industrial areas of high priority. Expansion of existing units has been liberalised and investment in moderanisation/renovation/replacement as well as export production, has been exempted from industrial licensing. Licensing of new capacity has been liberalised and concept of minimum economic scale introduced to promote production efficiency, taking advantage of economics of scale.

A number of policy measures have been initiated for development of specific industries like textiles, sugar, steel, electronics, etc. Steps have also been taken to tackle the problem of industrial sickness. These include (i) system for early detection of industrial sickness introduced by Reserve Bank of India' (ii) various steps for checking industrial sickness and promoting industrial revival evolved by Industrial Reconstruction Bank of India; (iii) setting up of Board for Industrial and Financial rreconstruction, and (iv) setting up of Small Industries Development Fund in IDBI to provide refinancing assistance not only for development, expansion and modernisation but also for rehabilitation of sick industrial units in small scale sector. The statement on industrial policy announced in July 1991 is being implemented. The new industrial policy emphasises delicensing and technological dynamism. Government has also set up modernisation funds for textiles and jute industries to cater to problems of those industries which account for major share of industrial sickness.

The Government is to establish 70 growth centres to act as a nucleus for industrial growth and promote accelerated development especially in backward areas. Sixty nine centres have already been identified. The process of setting up of the growth centres has been started. There has been an important milestone in the public sector steel capactiy with most of the main units of the Stage-I of the Visakhapatnam Steel Plant having come on stream in 1990-91. The 4 MT expansion programmes of Bhillai Steel Plant and Bokaro Steel Plant have also fully materialised during the year.

Technical advice and assistance to small scale manufacturers is provided by the Small Industries Development Organisation through its network of 16 service institutes, 16 branch institutes, 58 extension, production and training centres. The organisation also provides common service and tool room facilities in workshops attached to small industries, service institutes and extension centres. It conducts courses in management and technical disciplines. During 1974-75, it provided technical assistance to 1,02,684 entrepreneurs and visited 70,965 factories for spot guidance.

Two new centres namely the Central Insititute of Tool Design, Hyderabad, and The Institute for Design of Electrical Measuring Instruments, Bombay, have started providing technical guidance and training for entrepreneurs.

The National Small Industries Corporation, which was set up in 1955, operates the scheme of procuring machinery for small-scale manufacturers on a hire-purchase basis on concessional terms. The value of machines delivered under this scheme during the period April-October 1974 was Rs. 5.69 crores as against Rs. 3.25 crores during the corresponding period of the previous year. It also assists the small-scale sector in processing orders from government departments and agencies. The value of stores purchased by the Directorate General of Supply and Disposals from April to November 1974 was about Rs. 37 crores. The Prototype Development and Training Centres set up with American, West German and Japanese assistance at Rajkot, Okhla (Delhi) and Howrah impart training to persons engaged in small-scale industries.

Hitherto the emphasis was minly on agro-based industries. The growth of these industries was no doubt important for providing a ready market to the agricultural outputs, to create employment opportunities in view of seasonal nature of agriculture and to stabilise the farmer's income. Several specialised agencies such as the State Finance Corporations, Small Scale Reserve Bank, and the various technical guidance and assistance schemes of the Central Government, State Governments, Reserve Bank and State Bank of India were directed mainly to sustain the growth of small scale and cottage industries.

It was, however, realised at a later stage that the institutional at the "output" end is only one part of the game. Indian agriculture does not face any serious problem from the demand side. It is with the improvement in the technique of production that the cost of farming can be reduced and the productivity of the land can be improved in order to meet ever growing demandof agricultural outpout from direct consumers as well as from industries. The institutional set-up was, therefore, geared up to discover means for improving the technique of agricultural production and also to manufacture agriculture machinery.

At the highest level various agricultural research centres, headed by Indian Council of Agriculture Research, are performing important functions in the development and distribution of scientific knowledge of agriculture. There is also the Indian Society of Agriculture Engineers which provides a wealth of information for the application of science and technology to farming. At the village level cooperative societies are propagating and, where possible, implementing, the programmes of the research centres.

Cooperative societies and various official organisations have performed important functions but because of their limitations, these agencies could not meet the requirements of mechanised agriculture which has recetly gained importance for improving agricultural productivity.

Thus woith a view to meeting the rapidly growing demand of farmers for standard agricultural machinery equipment, e.g., tractors, power tillers, power threshers, seed-cum-fertilisers, drills, power sprayers and dusters, diesel and electric pump-sets, on cash or hire-purchase basis, the State Agro-Industrial Corporations have been established by the Government.

These corporations have been established in almost all the states. They are performing multifarious activities connected with not only the supply of agricultural machinery but also providing credit for the purpose. Some of them have ambitious programmes of designing and assembling tractors and manufacturing various tools and implements. But in fairness to the Corporations it must be recorded that none of them is more than three years old. What is more, some of them have the right ideas. In Gujarat, for instance, the AIC has decided to accord priority to the setting up of new cold storage plants in Banaskantha and Balsar, onion dehydration plants at Jamnagar and Bhavnagar and hydrogenated oil unit in the Saurashtra region. In West Bengal, the AIC will supply diesel pumping sets to poor farmers owning two to five acres of land on payment of Rs. 70 cash down, the balance of the price–Rs. 3,500–being recoverable in easy instanlments. In Tamil Nadu the AIC is not only going into the processing and marketing of farm produce but will also set up factories for the servicing and repair of the 1,000 new tractors which are sold in the state every year.

It is evidnt that the growth of agro-industries cannot reverse the process of urbanisation. Most of the plants for processing farm products or "waste" materials released by the existing agro-based industries like textiles must be established near the consuming centres if they are to pave their way. All that can be done in the circumstances is to establish new industrial units, both big and small, in district towns and away from the major cities. Any effort to confine the new agro-industries to the rural or semi-urban areas is bound to hinder their growth and will in the end be self-defeating.

Since there are quite a number of common problems which these institutions are likely to face, it might be worthwhile to establish a Central Agro-Industrial Corporation of India to coordinate the work of these state institutions. Besides coordinating the working of the state corporations, the central organisation can be entrusted with research and development of technology. Centralisation of research will eliminate waste and duplication. The State Corporations will, however, continue to collect data rom their regional offices to make them available to the central organisation. It will also be the task of the cental agency to arrange the production of different components of machinery and implements in different areas according to the local facilities available on the "comparative cost" basis. The proposed corporation can also serve as an effective agency in arranging the colllection of technical knowledge from abroad and distribution of imported machinery.

The massive expenditure that the Government has incurred on agricultural development has in one way or another gone to prop up a new rich class by passing millions of small farmers and landless labourers. There are growing indications of discontent among those who have found the cost of acquiring modern equipment and agricultural inputs soaring, on the one hand, and official and somehow getting channelled away from them, on the other.

The Government's decision to establish 500 pilot agro-service centres in the country is a step in the right direction. The programme is being jointly sponsored by the Ministry of Agriculture and the Ministry of Industrial Development and is designed to provide a wide range of services from custom-hiring of tractors and other farm equiptment and repair and maintenance of agricultural machinery to soil testing, crop spraying, water anaylsis and land and field services such as levelling and contour surveying. The scheme is intended to provide employment in the rural area as well as to accelerate the process of modernisation in the villages. It is particularly aimed at providing help to the small farmers and the weaker sections of the rural community in the relatively backward areas. The rapid increase in the use of tractors, pumps, mechanical threshers and other machines, not to speak of community radios, transistors and other personal gadgetry, has created a demand for easily available repair and maintenance facilities on a wide scale. Then agro-service centres can perform a valuable function provided they are suitably staffed and have the requisite managerial competence. The Government has negotiated World Bank assistance for tractor-cum-groundwater development projects in Punjab, Haryana and Tamil Nadu. Agro-service centres could be established alongside these programmes for a start.

As far as mechanical equipment like tractors and pumps are concerned, it would be most' desirable for the country to standardise on a few broad categories (not necessarily makes) so that problems of maintenance and the stocking of parts and components are not needlessly complicated by type differences. Little thought appears to have been given to this matter so far. But it is obviously something that calls for an early policy consideration.

Revenue

Direct taxes play a significant role in the tax system not only as a revenue source but as a powerful instrument for achieving social and economic objectives. Firstly, direct taxes help make tax systemprogressive and reduce disparities in distribution of income and wealth. Secondly, they subserve the strategy of planning in many ways. Differential taxation of savings in specified assets helps promote savings and induce flow of investment into desirable channels. In India, both income tax as well as taxes on capital, are designed to serve these objectives. The Income Tax Department administers a number of direct taxes Acts, namely, the Income Tax Act, 1953 (discontinued in respect of death on or after 16 March 1985); the Companies (Profit) Surtax Act, 1964 (discontinued from 1 April 1988); The Hotel Receipts Tax Act, 1987.

The Budget presented in 1995 has sought to accelerate the pace of reforms and modernisation of the Indian direct tax system that began three years ago. Some of the Important steps taken in that direction include tax incentives to boost up infrastructure development, expansion of the tax base by enlarging the scope of withholding of taxes, for the rationalisation of the tax structure and measures to combat black money by introduction of special procedure for speedy assessment in search cases.

The Income Tax Department is continously taking necessary legislative and administrative steps from time to time to curb/control black money and is also striving to check tax evasion and accumulation of unaccounted wealth. In pursuance of this objective, systematic surveys, search and seizure operations, verification of information by Central Information Branches in a planned manner and scrutiny of selected cases are undertaken. Persons found to be indulging in tax evasion are dealt with severely by inposing penalties and by launching prosecution proceedings against them.

Customs and Central exercise are the two important sources of the Central Government tax revenue. Revenue collection from Union Excise Duties (excluding cesses administered by other departments) upto December 1994 was Rs. 26,333.62 crore (provisional). While the revenue from Customs duties at the same time was Rs. 18,694.20 crore (provisional). The major policy steps taken towards simplication of excise taxation in 1994-95 ; budget were: (a) The reduction in the number of ad valorem rates to about half the existing number for simplicity and transparency; (b) Reduction in the dispersal of rates in each Chapter of Tariff; (c) Reduction in the number of exemption notifications to about half; (d) Shift in the bulk of excise taxation from secific to ad valorem rates to ensure built in buoyancy of revenues; (e) Continuing the process of lowering rates when they are unduly high; (f) Removal of complicated price list procedure; (g) Extension of modvat to capital goods, petroleum goods and spun yarns. The exercise of the tax reform initiated in Budget 1991-92 was continued in the Budget 1994-95 for simplification of the tax structure and movemnet towards moderate rates of taxation. The main features of customs tariff reform were: (i) The Maximum rate of Customs Duty was reduced to 65 per cent with the exception of passengers baggage, liquor, dried grapes, almonds, ball and roller bearings; (ii) The Customs Duty on Capital goods was further reduced to 25 per cent to boost investment to help domestic capital goods industry; (iii) substantial reduction in the duties on key raw materials, such as steel and chemicals; (iv) Reduction or removal of anomalies caused by important duties on raw materials and components being higher than on finished products; and (v) Elimination of the notification governing the administration of customs duties, thus reducing discretionary power and possibilities for disputes.

India is the largest producer and exporter of opium in the world. Cultivation of poppy and production and export of opium are under exclusive control of the Central Government. Control over opium cultivation have been made stricter inter alia by raising the minimum qualifying yield of opium for grant of licences for the crop year 1994-95 to 43 kg/hectare for the states of Madhya Pradesh, Uttar Pradesh and Rajasthan. A scheme of rewarding the cultivators who tendered higher yields was also intoduced. During 1993-94, India had exported about 619 metric tonnes of opium against production of 416 metric tonnes.

Drive against smugglers, tax evaders and drug traffickers was persued by strengthening of intelligence network and special attention to vulnerable areas. The year 1994-95 has also seen continuing efforts at better coordination with the intelligence and enforcement agences in India and other countries. Post seizure operation like preventive detention, under cofeposa in cases warranting such action, prosecution and adjudication etc., continued to receive special attention.

In addition to tackling of outright smuggling of contraband goods, customs authorities took strict action against certain companies in the organised sector indulging in tax evasion, import frauds, misues of duty exemption scheme, evasion of customs and excise duties and foreign exchange violations. As a result of vigorous anti-smuggling drive during 1994 goods worth Rs. 535.21 crore were seized.

Sales Tax is the most important source of revenue of the states. Levy of taxes on sale or purchase of goods taking place within a state is a state subject. Administration of the Central Sales Tax Act, 1956, under which tax is levied on inter-state sale of goods has been entrusted by law to the state governments who collect and retain the proceeds of such tax. Total collection of Sales Tax covering Central Sales Tax, tax on motor spirit and purchase tax on sugarcane during 1994-95 is estimated at Rs. 32,266.3 crore. Total collection of additional excise duty in lieu of sales tax during 1994-95 on sugar, tobacco and textiles is estimated at Rs. 2,725 crore.

Public debt

Public debt includes internal debt comprising borrowings inside the country like market loans, compensations and other bonds, treasury bills issued to the Reserve Bank of India, state governments, commercial banks and other parties as well as non-negotiable non-interest bearing rupees securities issued to the international financial institutions; and external debt comprising loans from foreign countries, international financial institutions etc. The "other liabilities" include outstanding against the various small saving schemes, provident funds, securities issued to Industrial Development Bank of India, Unit Trust of India and nationalised banks, deposits under the special deposit schemes, reserve funds and deposits.

Banking

Although some form of banking, mainly, money-lending type, has been in existence in India from ancient times, it was only little over a century ago that modern banking took its birth. the earlist institutions which undertook banking business under the British regime were agency houses which carried on banking business, in addition to their trading activities. Most of these agency huses were closed down during 1929-32. A number of banks which came into existence between the thirties and forties of the last century were also in great trouble. Prominent among these were three presidency banks which were later amalgamated into Imperial Bank of India in 1919 following a banking crisis.

The first bank of limited liability managed by Indians was Oudh Commercial Bank founded in 1881. Subsequently the Punjab National Bank was established in 1894. Swadeshi movement which began in 1906 encouraged the formation of a number of commercial banks. Banking crisis in 1913-1917 and failure of 588 banks in various states during the decade ending in 1949, underlined the need for regulating and controlling commercial banks. The Banking Companies (Inspection Ordinance) was passed in January 1946 and the Banking Companies (Restriction of Branches). Act in February 1946. The Banking Companies Act was passed in February 1949 which was subsequently amended to read as Banking Regulation Act. With a view to bringing commercial banks into the mainstream of economic development with definite social obligations and objective, Government issued an Ordinance on 19 July 1969 acquiring ownership and control of 14 major banks in the country, eith deposits exceeding Rs 50 crore each. Six more commercial banks were nationalised from 15 April 1980.

The objectives of public sector banking system were outlined on 21 July 1969. Some of them are to: (a) mobilise savings of people to the largest possible extent and utilise them for productive purposes; (b) operations of banking system should be promoted by a larger social purpose and should be subject to close public regulation; (c) cater to the legitimate credit needs of private sector industry and trade, big or small; (d) ensure that needs of productive sectors of the economy and in particular those of farmers, small scale industrialists and self-employed professional groups are met in an increasing manner; (e) nationalised banks to actively foster the growth of the new and progressive entrepreneurs and create fresh opportunities for hitherto neglected and backward areas in different parts of the country and (f) to curb the use of bank credit for speculative and other unproductive purposes.

Planning

Planning in India derives its objectives and social promises from Directive principles of State Policy enshrined in the Constitution. Public and private sectors are viewed as complementary. Private sector covers not only organised industry but also small scale industries, agriculture, trade and a great deal of activity in housing, construction and other fields. Individual effort and private initiative are considered necessary and desirable in national endeavour on development with optimkum of voluntary cooperation. Although in the past, economic planning did envisage a growing public sector with massive investments in basic and heavy industries, now the emphasis on the public sector is less pronounced and the current thinking on planning in the country, in general, is that it should increasingly be of an indicative nature.

Planning Commission was set up in 1950 to prepare the blue-print of development, taking an overall view of the needs and resources of the country.

The First Plan (1951-56) had a two fold objective to correct the disequilibrium in economy caused by the Second World War and partition of the country and also to initiate simultaneously a process of all-round balanced development. This was ensure increase in the national income and steady improvement in living standards. Keeping in view large-scale imports of foodgrains in 1951 and inflationary pressure on economy, the Plan accorded the highest priority to agriculture including irrigation and power projects. About 44.6 per cent of the total outlay of Rs. 2,069 crore in the public sector (later raised to Rs. 2,378 crore) was allotted for its development. The Plan also aimed at increasing the rate of investment from five to about seven per cent national income.

In 1954, Parliament decleared that the broad objectives of economic policy should be to achieve a 'socialistic pattern of society' under which the basic criteria for determining the lines of advance would be social gain and greater equality in income and wealth and not private profit. The Second Five Year Plan (1956-57 to 1960-61), therefore, sought to promote a pattern of development which sould ultimatley lead to the establishment of a socialistic pattern of society in India. In particular, it stressed that the benefits of economic development should accrue more to the relatively less privileged sections of society and there should be a progressive reduction in the concentration of incomes, wealth and economic power.

The main aims of the Second Plan were: (i) an increase of 25 per cent in the national income; (ii) rapid industrialisation with particular emphasis on the development of basic and heavy industries; (iii) large expansion of employment opportunities; and (iv) reduction of inequalities in income and wealth and more even distribution of economic power. The Plan also aimed at increasing the rate of investment from about seven per cent of the national income to 11 per cent 1960-61. The Plan laid special stress on industrialisation, increased production of iron and steel, heavy chemicals including nitrogenous fertilizers and development of heavy engineering and machine-building industry.

The Third Plan (1961-62 to 1965-66) aimed at securing a marked advance towards self-sustaining growth. Its immediate objectives were to: (i) secure an increase in the national income of over five per cent annum and at the same time ensure a pattern of investment which could sustain this rate of growth during subsequent Plan periods; (ii) achieve self-sufficiency in foodgrains and increase agricultural production to meet the requirements of industry and exports; (iii) expand basic industries like steel, chemicals, fuel and power and to establish machine-building capacity, so that the requirements of further industrialisation could be met within a period of 10 years or so mainly from the country's own resources; (iv) utilise fully the manpower resources of the country and ensure substantial expansion in employment opportunities; and (v) establish progresively greater equality of opportunity and bring about reduction in disparities of income and wealth and a more even distribution of economic power. The Plan aimed at increasing the national income by about 30 per cent from Rs. 14,500 crore in 1960-61 to about Rs. 19,000 crore by 1965-66 (at 1960-61 prices) and per capita income by about 17 per cent from Rs. 330 to Rs. 385 during the same period.

The situation created by the Indo-Pakistan conflict in 1965, two successive years of severe drought, devaluation of the currency, general rise in prices and erosion of resources available for Plan purposes delayed finalisation of the Fourth Five Year Plan. Instead, between 1966 and 1969, three Annual Plans were formulated within the framework of the draft outline of the Fourth Plan. They took into account the conditions prevailing at that time. The state of the economy and the non-availablity of financial resources for Plan purposes kept down the size of development outlay during this period.

The Fourth Plan (1969-74) aimed at accelerating the tempo of development and reducing fluctuations in agricultural production as well as a the impact of uncertainties of foreign aid. It sought to raise the standard of living through programmes designed to promote equality andsocial justice. The Plan laid particular emphasis on improving condition of less privileged and weaker sections especially through provision of employment and education. Efforts were also directed towards reduction of concentration and wider diffusion of wealth, income and economic power.

The Plan aimed at inincreasing net domestic production at 1968-69 factor cost from Rs. 29,071 crore in 1969-70 to Rs. 38,306 crore in 1973-74. In terms of 1960-61 prices, this implied an increase from Rs. 17,351 crore in 1968-69 to Rs. 22,862 crore in 1973-74. Average annual compound rate of growth envisaged was 5.7 per cent.

The Fifth Plan (1974-79) was formulated against the backdrop of severe inflationary pressures. Major objectives of the Plan were to achieve self-reliance and adopt measures for raising consumption standards of people living below the poverty line. This Plan also gave high priority to bring inflation under control and to achieve stability in the economic situation. It targeted an annual growth rate of 5.5 per cent in national income. Four Annual Plans pertaining to the Fifth Plan period were completed. It was subsequently decided to end the Fifth Plan with the close of Annual Plan 1978-79 and initiate work for a new Plan for next five years with new priorities and programmes.

The Sixth Plan (1980-85) was conceptualised keeping in view achievements and shortcomings of the past three decades of planning. Removal of poverty was foremost objective of the Plan even though it was recognised that task of this magnitude could not be accomplished in a short period of five years. The strategy adopted for the Plan consisted essentially in moving simultaneously towards strengthening infrastructure for both agriculture and industry so as to create conditions for an accelerated growth in investments, output and exports and provide through special programmes designed for the purpose, increased opportunities for employment especially in rural areas and unorganised sector and as well meeting minimum basic needs of people. Stress was laid on dealing with inter-related problems through a system approach rather than in separate cmpartments, greater management efficiency and intensive monitoring in all sectors and active involvement of people in formulating specific schemes of development at local level and securing their speedy and effective implementation

Sixth Plan's actual expenditure stood at Rs. 1,09,291.7 crore (current prices) as against the envisaged total public sector outlay of Rs. 97,500 crore (1970-80 prices) accounting for a 12 per cent increase in nominal terms. Average annual growth rate for the Plan was 5.2 per cent, targeted growth rate for this period.

The Seventh Plan (1985-90) emphasised on Policies

and programmes, the aim of which had been rapid growth in foodgrains production production, employment opportunities and productivity within the framework of basic tenets of planning, namely, growth, modernisation, self-relience and social justice. Due to overall fovourable weather conditions, implementation of various thrust programmes and with concerted efforts of the government and the farmers, foodgrains production during the Seventh Plan grew by 3.23 per cent as compared to along term growth rate of 2.68 per cent during 1967-68 to 1988-89 and a growth rate of 2.255 per cent in eighties. To reduce unemployment and, consequently, the incidence of poverty, special programmes like Jawahar Rozgar Yojana were initiated in addition to the already existing programmes. Due recognition was also accorded to the role small scale and food-processing industries can play in this regard. Various policy instruments were used to improve the productivity and the international competitiveness of the Indian economy. Instead of creating new facilities, the thrust was on improvement of existing facilities, and fuller capacity utilisation.

The total expenditure during the entire Seventh Plan stood at Rs. 2,18,729.62 crore (current price) as against the envisaged total public sector outlay of Rs. 1,80,000 crore, resulting in a 21.52 per cent increase in nominal terms. During this Plan period, Gross Domestic product (GDP) grew at an average rate of 5.6 per cent per year exceeding the targeted growth rate by 0.6 per cent

The Eight Five Year Plan (1990-95) could not take off due to the fast changing political situation at the Centre. The new government which assumed power at the Centre by June 1991 decided that the Eighth Five Year Plan would commence on 1 April 1992 and that 1990-91 and 1991-92 should be treated as separate Annual Plans. Formulated within the framework of the earlier Approach to the Eighth Five Year Plan (1990-95), the basic thrust of these Annual Plans were on maximisation of employment and social transformation.

The Plan proposes a growth rate of 5.6 per cent per annum on an average during the Plan period. The level of national investment is proposed at Rs. 7,98,000 crore and the public sector outlay of Rs. 4,34,100 crore. Consistent with the expected resource position, the size of the plans of the states and union territories is projected at Rs. 1,86,235 crore and of the Central Plan at Rs. 2,47,865 crore.

The Annual Plan 1992-93 envisaged a total public sector outlay of Rs. 80,771.96 crore, actual expenditure came down to Rs. 72,853 crore which is lower by one per cent than the Budget Estimates for the Plan. The actual size of the Plans for states and union territories was lower by nearly 10 per cent i.e. from Rs. 32,364.88 crore (BE) to Rs. 29,159 crore. The main reasons for the shortfall in State Plans were deterioration in the balance from current revenues, erosion in the contribution of state electricity boards and in some cases of state road transport corporations, negative opening balances,mounting non-plan expenditure, shortfalls in the collection of small savings, etc.

The envisaged total public sector outlay of Rs. 1,00,120.16 crore for the Annual Plan 1993-94 on revision came down to Rs. 92,623.64 crore which is lower by 7.48 per cent that the budget estimates for the Plan. In the Central Sector, the approved outlay was Rs. 61,453.53 crore. The total outlay of the plans for states and union territories on revision was lower by 13.84 per cent i.e. from Rs. 36,184 crore in the budget estimates to Rs. 31,175.11 crore in revised estimates. The main reasons for the shortfall in states plans were deteriorating in the balance from current revenues, erosion in the contribution of state electricity boards and in some cases of state road transport corporations, negative opening balances, mounting non-plan expenditure, shortfall in the collection of small savings, etc.

The Annual Plan 1994-95 provides for a public sector outlay of Rs. 1,12,197 crore at current prices. At 1991-92 prices it would be about 20 per cent of the envisaged Eighth Plan public sector outlay. The state plans outlay is Rs. 39,992 crore at current prices, which works out to 35.64 per cent of public sector outlay and 17.17 per cent of the Eighth Plan provision for the states at 1991-92 prices. In the first three years, assuming that the actual outlays will be the same as the revised estimates of 1993-94 and the budget estimates of 1994-95 will be reallised, the public sector outlays in the Central Plan and the State Plans will work out to 59 per cent and 44 per cent of the respective Eighth Plan provisions, at constant prices.

An era of planning thus started in 1951, when the First Five Year Plan was launched. This was followed by the Second Five Year Plan (1955-56) and the Third Five Year Plan (1960-61). All these developments, from the Grow More Food Campaign in 1942 to the planned economy, are discussed separately. On the whole, the country lacked any well-defined policy of agriculture up to the end of Second Five Year Plan. Many improvements have taken place since then.

Cooperative farming, declared at one stage as the ultimate form of organisation for agricultural production, did not receive wide acceptance and that accounts for lack of any serious effort or enthusiastic response to its implementation. To achieve social justice, ceiling on the size of holdings is being imposed but there is considerable confusion in matters of detail and execution. Adequate investigations are lacking to justify the measure economically. There is good cultivable land which is lying waste in some states not because the ownership rights are vested in persons who are not able to farm it themselves but also because they do not lease it out for fear of losing their title to it. To the extent such land is brought under cultivation, the measure may prove beneficial. But where the holdings are pushed down below a certain minimum size, it is not easy to predict the effect on agricultural efficiency and production.

Quite often the emphasis on increasing the production of foodgrains has led to a fall in the production of commercial crops, leading to shortage of such products. In turn a cry is raised to increase the production of cash crops. Such an action can hardly be called a policy. Not much thought was given to preparing the estimates of cost-benefit ratio in undertaking programmes of large-scale irrigation and land reclamation. Therefore, emhasis has been changing from major to minor irrigation projects and vice versa; similarly from land reclamation to raising the standard and intensity of cultivation on land already under the plough.

These instances make it clear that hardly any well-defined policy existed and much less was pursued. A sound policy calls for precise and detailed information on cost-benefit relationships of various developmental projects, efficiency standards, and farms in various size groups in different farming type regions. First, it is necessary to have a census of agricultural resources, surveys on land use, investigations on factors inhibiting agricultural efficiency regionwise and the demand projections for the current and future needs in respect of food, cash crops, and export. Then taking the country and regions as units, sound plans need to be drawn up for land use, agricultural production, and needed supplies. To support the fulfilment of these targets, ancillary measures need be taken, namely, land reclamation, assistance in raising the intensity of cultivation, credit support, educational programmes, irrigation, etc. All such measures, for successful implementation, need a watchdog in the form of adequate farm management and agricultural economics research to guide and evaluate simultaneously the execution of the programmes in order to make them efficient and effective and to stop those measures which, on experience, have a retrograde effect.

No doubt, steps have been taken towards the direction suggested above, the major lacunae in them may be listed as follows:

— The carrying out of developmental activities on a piecemeal basis with the result that full benefits expected from such programmes have not been obtained. In UP, tube-wells, for example, were dug but could not be commissioned for lack of energisation.

— The budgetary provision for efforts in various directions were made on the basis of administrative divisions and not on a properly estimated requirement of expenditure with the consequence that the efforts were too thinly spread and proved almost futile. The early Grow More Food Campaign is an appropriate example of this.

— The approach where an investment could be most effective from the point of view of natural factors like land, climate or economic factors like demand, particularly in the case of livestock products, has been conspicuous by its absence.

— Duplication and overlapping has often led to futility of efforts which cold never be enough according to needs and urgency.

If we examine any one of the policy measures on prices of foodgrains, production, distribution, land tenure, irrigation, land reclamation and settlement, we will see that each one has some woeful tale to tell. In the functions of the Ministry of Community Development and Cooperation and the Ministry of Agriculture, there was a considerable overlapping till they were recently merged. Between them and even within the same ministry there is duplication of positions. This leads not only to wastage of scarce funds but also to confusion in working.

A number of committees have from time to time gone into the problem of agricultural administration and machinery. All of them have helped to expand agricultural organisation. Mention may be made of the Patel Committee (1945-46) as a result of whose recommendations the Directorate of Economics and Statistics became a separate unit of the Ministry; the enquiry by N. Gopalsawami Ayyanger (1949), which recommended the creation of the Bureau of Natural Resources and Agriculture with a coordinating minister for the Ministries of Agriculture, Food and works; the W.R. Natu Enquiry 1951; and more recently the enquiry Mr. Keifer (1965). Full-scale general enquiries have also been made of the machinery of the Government of India leading to proposals for its reorganisation by Richard Tottenham in 1945, by Shri R.A. Gopalsawami in 1952 and Dr. Appleby in 1954. It may also be mentioned here that the Food Grains Policy Committee, 1947, the Grow More Food Committee 1952 and the Balwantrai Mehta Committee, 1957 also have made recommendations for the reorganisation of the machinery of agricultural administration at different levels. The desire for administrative improvement has been continuous, the suggestions for reform numerous, but the practical results of the enquiries have been rather disappointing.

Piecemeal changes and adjustments have been made from time to time. There has been some bureau shuffling off and on but no thorough reorganisation that could assure the efficient functioning of the machinery for accelerating development.

Agriculture

In order to streamline agricultural production in the country, an Agricultural Board was constituted in 1963. The main function of the Board was to bring about expenditious implementation of the programme for the development of agriculture including animal husbandry, forestry and fisheries. The working of the board was recently reviewed and the Minister of Food, Agriculture, Community Development and Cooperation is its Chairman and the Minister of State in the Ministry of Finance, and the Member Agriculture, Planning Commission, are its members. The function and powers of the board are: (i) to secure effective and continuous coordination between the Centre and the states, in matters relating to the formulation and execution of development programmes; (ii) to review the progress of development programmes, ensure efficient arrangements for supplies and services, locate difficulties, if any, and endeavour to remove them; and (iii) to take such other measures as would ensure speedy and effective implementation of the development programmes at the Centre and in the states. The decisions of the Board will be treated as the decisions of the Government of India as long as they are within the plan provisions and within the framework of the approved budget provisions of the ministries concerned.

The Ministry of Agriculture was reorganised in 1964 on the initiative of the then Minister of Food and Agriculture who had found it a poor instrument for carrying out a dynamic and forward-looking policy aimed at making the country self-sufficient and even surplus in the foodgrains and assuring the prosperity of the farming population. The reorganisation was aimed at making the Ministry "function more effectively and to enable it more actively to associate itself with the implementation of development schemes by the states." It attempted (i) a redistribution of subjects and responsibilities among the various units of the Ministry so as to make the assignments of the units compact and specific; (ii) to assign to scientific and technical officers of the Ministry executive functions and operational responsibilities for planning, implementation and supervision of programmes, in addition to their advisory functions, to secure through "better administrative machinery"; and (iii) closer and more continuous contact between the Central and State Governments in the implementation of agricultural plan schemes and to improve Centre-State relations.

The apex of the structure of administration consists of the Minister of Food and Agriculture, who is a senior member of the Cabinet, and Ministers of State and Deputy Ministers who constitute the political executive. The Secretary of the Ministry is the official head of the Ministry and the principal adviser to the Minister. The Department of Agriculture which is one of the three departments included in the Ministry is organised in eight wings, and has besides five specialised offices, a number of supervisory and operational agencies and some cells and units for certain specific purposes.

The eight wings of the department are: (1) Production; (2) Forestry; (3) Fisheries; (4) Inputs (F) (Fertilisers); (5) Inputs (M) (Machinery); (6) Land problems; (7) Special development programmes; and (8) Coordination. The specialised of offices are: (1) The Indian Council of Agricultural Research; (2) The Directorate General of State Farms; (3) Agricultural Prices

Commission; (4) The Directorate of Extension; and (5) The Directorate of Economics and Statistics.

Lastly, reference may be made to the numerous subordinate and attached offices of the Department which operate various programmes of the Ministry, expert committees and other agencies. The more important attached offices are the Directorate of Plant Protection, the Office of the Agricultural Marketing Advisor, the National Seeds Corporation, the Warehousing Corporation, etc.

Committees, both official and unofficial, expert or representative of interests, have been established to advise the Ministry on many important matters. Fifteen of these have been listed as functioning at present. These are Panel of Economists, Panel of Experts on Agricultural Demonstration and finally Panel of Farmers to advise the Agricultural Prices Commission.

The other agencies falling in this category are: Committee for the Improvement of Agricultural Statistics; National Committee on the Preparation of Farm Management; Manual for the use of Extension Workers; Study Group on Wild Life and Wild Life Products; Indian Board for Wild Life; Central Forestry Commission; Board for Agricultural Machinery and Implements; Standing Committe of Experts on Manures and Fertilisers; National F.A.O. Liaison Committee; Central Council of Gosamvardhana; Central Variety Release Committee; Central Board of Fisheries; and Central Fisheries Research Committee.

The areas covered by these boards and committees are of vital importance to the development of agriculture and it is necessary, therefore, that they should be active bodies manned by competent personnel.

The Planning Commission's role in agricultural administration needs to be examined. It is directly and intimately connected with agricultural development at all stages from policy formulation and planning to plan implementation and evaluation. The Planning Commission's concurrence is required for the ministry's policies and programmes in detail. In fixing the targets of production, in making financial allocations in the five year plan and in the annual plans, in negotiations with the states, the Planning Commission plays a leading, if not dominant role. The working relations between the Planning Commission and the Ministry have not been always smooth and are not infrequently marked by friction.

Multi-Level planning and programme implementation

Apex-planning body at state level is generally state Planning board comprising chief minister as chairman and finance and planning ministers of the state and some technical experts as members. Department of planning in state government provides secretariat for the board. In many states, planning process has been decentralised to district level and in some states even to sub-division or block levels. In most of the states, there is district planning committee or district planning council comprising both official and non-official members. Some states also have a separate set-up consisting of functionaries like district planning officers, economist, credit planners, project appraiser, export training coordinator and an area planner in some of the districts for formulation of district plans, which are integrated with state plan.

The Seventy Third and Seventy Fourth Constitutional Amendment Acts are the culmination of the evolutionaly process as far as secentralisation of democratic power is concerned. With passing of appropriate legislations by the state governments and the conduct of elections to the panchayati raj institutions,

Zilla parishads, Nagar Palika, etc. will be empowered to plan, fund and implement appropriate developmental works at the local level.

The Ministry of Programme Implementation (now Department of Programme implementation in the MInistry of Planning and Programme Implementation) was set up in September 1985 to usher in a new system of goaloriented management to closely monitor implementation of anti-poverty programmes, performance of all industrial infrastructure sectors of economy and implementation of Central Sector industrial projects costing over Rs. 20 crore each. The Department through its efficient system, prompt facilitative action and computerised network provided by the National Informatics Centre, is ensuring effective implementation of projects and programmes.

Infrastructure Monitoring by the Department of Programme Implementation aims at reviewing the physical performance with reference to the targets for the financial year of nine industrial infrastructure sectors namely, power, coal, steel, railways, telecommunications, shipping and ports, fertilizers, cement and petroleum and natural gas, which have a pivotal role in the economic development of the nation. This involves identifying problem areas requiring action on a priority basis and coordinating the efforts of administrative ministries with a view to overcoming critical bottlenecks, determining intersectoral linkages for achieving optimal results with emphasis on better capacity utilisation.

Physical targets (for each area in respect of each infrastructure sector) are examined at the beginning of the year for knowing the overall growth in infrastructure performance from 1985-86 to 1994-95.

The present author conducted an awareness survey with the morning and evening walkers of Vaishali and district parks of Pitampura in Delhi. Most respondents were retired teachers, government officers, businessmen and youth.

The teachers who taught economics had a fairly good idea about plans but with the exception of three or four, none had cared to read even in the newspapers about the import of the Ninth Plan approach paper. Teachers belonging to the disciplines of literature such as Hindi, Sanskrit and English had very little idea of even the concept of 'plan'.

The businessmen were more concerned with their "self-interests" and profits rather than plan/s. "The plans were the concern of Tatas and Birlas. " They were primarily concerned with the yearly budget to adjust their business accordingly.

The government officers, who retired as section officers, were hardly aware of the plan. Of course, they were concerned with their pensions and closely followed the annual budget.

The youth had hardly any time to read newspapers except about vacancies. They seemed to be a frustrated lot!

In rural India, the condition is worse. Hardly anybody knows about the plans except some of the various schemes which were advantageous to them. The common man has no knowledge or information about the plans and programmes

Communication gap: In the absence of consciousness and awareness, it is extremely difficult to expect people to co-operate and participate in the schemes and programmes of plans. There appears to be a very big communication gap. In earlier times, "Planning Forums" in universities and colleges had made teachers and students aware of the plan/s. These should be revived. The teachers and students may take the message of plans to the people.

The funcftions of communication are, today, much wider. Besides, information and motivation, they include socialization which implies stimulation of people's active involvement in public issues. Communication has to be linked to people"s needs, both material and non-material, The mass-media, particularly the electronic media such as radio and television tend to claim a much higher degree of attention than the verbal media. This needs to be exploited fully.

Gandhi's theory of communication : Gandhi offers us a theory of non-violent communication which consists of four theoretical units. The first and foremost of theoretical units is non-violent speech and action; the second unit is the maintenance of relationships and enrichment of personality; and the third is openness; and the fourth is flexibility. Gandhi's theory of communication may be thought as instrumental in bringing about communal harmony and generating interest in the plan.

Kurukshetra : Journal of Ministry of Rural Areas and Employment can become an effective instrument of communication. Other journals such as Yojana can also play an active role in this respect.

Achievements and failures

Literacy: As per the 1991 census, the literacy rete in India was 52.11 per cent. The rate of literacy in urban male and female was 81 per cent and 63.9 per cent respectively, while in rural areas among males and females it was 57.8 per cent and 30.3 per cent respectively. The role of literacy among the Scheduled Castes and Scheduled Tribes women was pretty low i.e. 23.76 per cent and 18.19 per cent respectively.

In villages, the girl's education is far behind. If 100 girls take admision in the first grade, by the time they reach fifth standard only 40 girls remain; in the eighth standard only 18, in the 10th, 9 and only one in the twelfth standard. The picture changes radically in urban areas. There are 82 in the fifth, 62 in the eighth, 32 in the tenth and 14 in the twelfth standard.

Drinking water: There are 27 per cent villages and 21 per cent cities, where safe driking water is available. In 1,62,000 villages, no potable water is available as per the data obtained from government sources by 1993. In fact, there are 60 per cent villages which have no safe drinking water, while liquor shops are there in 90 per cent villaves.

Housing: There is a shortage of 13.7 million houses in villages according to 1991 census. The living conditions in 36 per cent in cities and 73 per cent in villages are extremely poor.

Link roads: As per oficial estimates, out of 1,29,852 villages with a population of 1,000 or more, 1,12,190 villages have links roads (1995-96). The late US President, John F. Kennedy once said : "It is not wealth that builds our roads but roads that build our wealth".

Availability of food: In 1991, per capita availability of food was 510 grams which has come down to 474.2 grams by 1994. Health: There are primary health centres in almost all the blocks of the country. Arrangement for a 30-bed hospital is made for a population of one lakh. Access to sanitation is available only to 16 per cent of the people of India.

The general difficulty recognized by all studies is that government schemes and programmes do not reach people for whom they are meant. The late Prime Minister Rajiv Gandhi had said that only 15 paise reach people out of the 100 earmarked. Thus the "citizen" is lost between leaders and bureaucrats.

Prof B.M. Bhatia says that vaious poplist programmes although thought of as poverty alleviating and job creation programmes, are in reality nothing more than vote catching devices used by politicians to keep themselves in power. And all this at the cost of the public exchequer. They are nothing but bribes to the voters for casting the vote in favour of ruling political party or parties which initiated the programes. It is time people understood that the public distribution system (PDS), dual pricing system, consumption articles, and running multitude of welfare schemes are all part of the game politicians play in a democracy. By coing so, they are promoting their own selfish interests, and by no means serving a public cause. The UF government, though in a minority in the Lok Sabha, has started giving the impression the it will act boldly in the matter. A Cabinet Minister said the other day: "We can's seconomy". This comes as a whiff of fresh air. Besides, he went on to add, "the previous...government which sougth to be populist and held back a price hike for petrol for three years and introduced a subsidy of Rs. 1,288 crore for sugar in 1992 could not come back to power".

Micro-level planning

The Planning Commission has indicated, in the Ninth Five Year Plan that the priorities for the public sector outlays are the seven basic minimum services that were identified and adopted by the Chief Ministers' conference of July, 1996 for attainment by AD 2000. It is believed that social development and rural development cannot take place in a noon-growth environment. Employment and social security are vital to social development. Hence, the focus of micro-planning is made on:

(i) Cent per cent coverage provision of safe drinking water in rural and urban areas;

(ii) Cent per cent coverage of primary health service facilities in rural and urban areas;

(iii) Universalization of primary education;

(iv) Provision of public housing assistance to all shelterless poor families;

(v) Extension of midday meal programme in primary schools to all rural blocks and urban slums disadvantaged sections;

(vi) provision of connectivity to all unconnected villages and habitations;

(vii) Streamlining the public distribution system with the focus on the poor;

(viii) Growth and growth-related infrastructure particularly power and irrigation;

(ix) Employment; and

(x) Social security.

Thus the seven basic minimum services, growth and growth-related infrastructure, employment and social security form the focus of micro-level planning.

Planning for and by the people: Two teams comprising officials and non-officials, visit the habitations and encourage people to participate in Shramdan and also apprise them of the need for and scope of micro-level planning. The teams also help the people to draw up their own plans in all the sectors which would reflected the vision of the villagers on different key areas in their ward, the desired and achievable goals in five years, the next one year and the next quarter. It indicates the specific action by the people and identify the assistance required from the government to achieve the goals set by them. Under this exercise, the students' team led by a lecture who is a group leader would act in close co-operation with the Sarpanch and the ward members, teachers and other village functionaries, youth clubs, literacy campaign volunteers, non-government organizations, women's groups, watershed committee members, Vana Samrakshana Samithi members et al. The micro-level plan so prepared would be handed over to the nodal officer for eventual transfer to the Gram Panchayat. It is the villagers who would implement the plan for themselves and by themselves and they could do so effectively. The implementation of the programme would be reviewed periodically.

Since the launching of the Janmabhoomi programme is the first of its kind in the country, the success of the programme would lead to further effective implementation of the micro-level planning in Andhra Pradesh as well as other States. Against this background, an effort is made in the present article to evaluate the Janmabhoomi programme in Cuddapah district of Andhra Pradesh.

The study was conducted in Cuddapah, a backward drought-prone district in the Rajyalaseema region of the State. Out of 50- Mandals, 20 were randomly selected for the present study. From each selected Mandal, a sample of 15 group leaders were drawn and the primary data was collected using a pre-structured scheduled besides discussions with the nodal officers, parents and political leaders.

The Janmabhoomi programme was launched in all 2,494 habitations in Cuddapah district. The programme also covered 22 slums in Cuddapah municipality and 29 slums in Proddatur municipality. As many as 2,682 Prajala Vaddaku Palana teams were formed in addition to 2,552 roup leaders comprising lecturers, headmasters and teachers. The notable feature was the voluntary involvement of 21,337 junior and degree college students including 2,680 girls in the programme. And, the youth, voluntary organizations, political parties and leaders also enthusiastically participated in the programme. The government officials and the school teachers functioned as 2,835 facilitators to provide the required facilities to the teams and to-co-ordinate the villagers and the teams.

The group leaders and students stayed in the habitations from January 1 to 8 to serve and motivate the villagers to participate in Shramdan and improve their surroundings. Emphasis was laid on providing clean drinking water, health and hygiene, environmental cleanliness, primary education and family planning and inculcating a sense of unity and self-reliance, and enlightened people on achieving development through a positive approach. Under the health package, vitamin A was administered to children under five years of age to prevent incidence of night blindness and iron and folic doses were given to check anaemia. All the eligible couples with two children were motivated to undergo sterilization and oral contraceptive were distributed to recently married couples. The Department of Agriculture and the District Rural Development Agency also prepared packages and propagated the rural development schemes.

In the Janmabhoomi programme, the institution of Gram Sabha played a prominent role. Gram Sabhas or village meetings were conducted in the evenings where various problems were discussed. Solutions were worked out besides preparation of micro-level planning of the habitation for the next three months, one year as well as the vision statement in respect of all the sectors for the next five-year period with the help of the Sarpanch and other leaders in the villages. The team not only prepared the actual planning on the basis of locally available resources but also helped the villagers in identifying the problem areas and in planning for remedial action or further progress in different key areas. Cleaning of school premises, clearance of thorny bushes, cleaning and upkeep of sanitation, maintenance of potable water, laying of roads, digging of soakpits near hand-pumps, repairing the bore wells, white washing of school and government buildings, plantation of trees, and repairs to irrigation canals were some of the important services renders by the teams in the villages with the active participation of the public. They also sensitized the villagers on issues like health, hygiene literacy, savings, environment, etc. Besides, the students surveyed the habitations under the supervision of their group leaders and collected all the details relating to literacy, size of family, drinking water, sanitation, health care, family planning, primary education, public distribution, power, transport, roads, communication, etc. which are evolved into basic data for the future planning of the habitation with allocations coming in the next budget.

Planning is not only an instrument of economic growth but it is accepted by all that it is an instrument of social integration. Indian society consists of many social groups both in caste, community and ethnic terms. During the national movement it was realized that political mobilization has to be done in the context of the castes and community terms. That is why Gandhi is known as a political fold. Their participation fold. Their participation in the political movement brought their economic and social needs into sharp focus. Any planning has to recognize their needs. As such, the Indian Donstitution has recognized these social groups. They are socially and economically backward. They do not have access to modern education and social services. Planning as a concept was developed during the national movement. The democratic experiment of India has to take into account the needs of SCs/STs and the OBCs. It is mandatory.

Reforms

Planning is an integral part of our political culture. Strengthening democracy is possible with planning,. Planning accepts the role of State in the market economy. The role of the State is to reduce the regional disparity. It is to reduce the income disparity between various sections of our society. Liberalization process has restricted the role of the State in the area of industrialization. The private capital is today strong enough to stand on its own feet. Withdrawing the State from economic activities is a welcome step. But historical experience of the Third World countries show that the first decade of economic liberalization generated lot of economic distress. The approach paper to the Ninth Five Year Plan document has recognized this new development.

First, the regional disparity between poorer regions and richer areas has increased. Regional disparity has created already a lot of political mobilization on ethnic line.

Secondly, investment in agriculture has slowed down during this phase which sustains a majority of our people to earn their livelihood. Even after 50 years of industrialization, our agriculture is not self-sustaining. It needs State intervention for its growth. The lack of agricultural growth has reduced the employment opportunities that is reflected in the rise of unemployment and underemployment in rural India and which has pushed them to overcrowd the cities. As a result, it has increased urban poverty. Both rural and urban poverty have a close relationship.

Thirdly, urban areas are facing the crisis, in terms of providing drinking water and sanitation where the urban poor are living.

Fourthly, the decade of economic liberalization has increased the number of poor, people below the poverty line. Who are these poor people in the rural areas and urban slums? They are nobody except the people from the SCs/STs and the lower OBCs. These social classes are today the worst victims of the economic process.

The approach paper to the Ninth Plan has looked into the factors explained in the above paragraphs. It demands the reorientation of the State role and definite thrust on the poverty alleviation and employment generation without which the poor are going to distrust the democratic system. Once alienation of these communities from the system starts growing, then the system itself is going to be vulnerable.

The year 1991 marks a watershed in the economic history of India, as the country went through a paradigm shift-from one of the most highly regulated economies of the world which was essentially inward-looking to a market-oriented system, reducing the role of Government in making economic decisions, as the means to achieve higher growth of the economy and its rapid integration with the rest of the world.

An economic stabilisation programme and structural reforms covering trade, industry, taxation, financial sector and capital market were put through turning the worst economic crisis that confronted India since Independence into an opportunity to usher in a quiet revolution which would enable the country to attain a trajectory of higher growth and, along with it, social equity.

Developments in the Gulf region in 1990 exerted pressures on India's balance of payments and with outflow of capital, mainly NRI deposits, the foreign exchange reserves declined to about one billion dollars (barely two weeks of imports) in June 1991. The country was for the first time on the verge of defaulting on its external debt. There was no choice but to have recourse to a structural adjustment programme with the International Monetary Fund providing a standby credit for a stabilisation programme coupled with wide-ranging reforms.

The first steps were in the area of Trade Policy by devaluing the rupee by 22 per cent in dollar terms, eliminating export subsidy and reducing import licensing restrictions. A dual exchange rate system was ushered in but by March 1993, it was unified and a fully floating exchange rate regime in which the exchange rate is determined by market forces of demand and supply came into being. The foreign exchange market was widened and deepened, and in August 1994, the rupee was made fully convertible on current account, trade and non-trade. The downward adjustment of the rupee was designed to improve the country's international competitiveness and correct the imbalances in trade and current accounts.

Beginning with the 1991-92 Budget, Government also launched a phased reduction of import tariff bringing down the maximum from 300 per cent in 1990 to 50 per cent by march 1995. The changes resulted in lowering the import-weighted average tariff from 87 per cent in 1991 to 27 per cent in March 1995. The dispersion of tariffs was also significantly reduced and quantitiative restrictions were substantially eased. The trade reforms undertaken from 1991 helped to reduce the anti-export bias of Indian industry which was being exposed to both domestic and international competition.

The thrust of the Export-Import Policy (1992-97), made coterminus with the Eighth Five year Plan, is export promotion which is crucial for balance of payment and at the same time the Policy facilitates the import of production inputs required for sustaining increased industrial growth and exports.

Exports have responded impressively to the policy reforms and after the slowdown in the first two years under the impact of macrostabilisation measures, grew by an average of 18-19 per cent in the subsequent three years (1993-94 to 1995-96) in dollar terms. Exports have now diversified both commoditywise and countrywise with an increasing share going to the rest of Asia, particularly East and South East Asia with which India is trying to evolve increased trade and investment cooperation, given the rapid growth and the dynamism of these economies.

India's exports have undoubtedly gained from the expansion in world trade-as will be seen from the fact that a slowdown in global exports in 1996 has also effected India's exports to some extent in the current year-but the Government is confident that the export target of 38 billion dollars in 1996-97 would be achieved as against the 31.8 billion in 1995-96. A target of 75 billion dollars of exports by 2,000 A.D. has been set and this would mean maintaining an annual export growth of around 20 per cent in dollar terms over the next four years. This would facilitate a steady rise in the ratio of exports and imports in GDP and take India closer to one per cent as its share of world trade by the year 2001. Changes in the direction of India's trade from 1960-61 are brought out in Table IV.

In recent years, a largest percentage of imports are covered by exports—88 per cent in 1995-96. Imports have also increased with industry stagin a strong recovery from 1993-94 onwards to record double digitrates of growth. The higher import bill also reflects the demand for mass consumption items like pulses and edible oils apart from the growing dependence on imports of petroleum crude and products to keep pace with the rapid growth in energy use in the country.

Local resource mobilization & local planning

Indeed at the local level, resources like land, labour and human and physical resources—physical capital to a limited extent are available. Techno—economic surveys can identify the potential resources. But will all the labour force be mobilized for gainful and productive employment? This is a more important task and accompllishing ths depends on the integration of the techno—economic approach with other aspect of the social system and development process. This is the concern of many mono—disciplines like economics, engineering, sociology, psychology, etc. All such studies have pointed out that only at the local level, the basic needs, particularly of vulnerable sections can be identified and they justify larger investment in primary education for promoting health, nutrition, rural development, family size, fertility, literacy and awareness of national culture.

It is true that rural development is in the main equivalent to the development of food and cash croops and their needed inputs—irrigation, fertilizer, seeds and other resource inputs–animal husbandry, dairying and poultry farming, fisheries, forestry and agro—industries. (Dr,. Malcolm S. Adisheshiah in Bulletin of Madras Institute of Development Studies, January 1991 P.41). But such investments in agricultural developmentare bound to be more effective when there is adequate investment in human resource development, particularly in literacy and primary education. Between the I and VII Five Year Plans, there has been a decline in agriculture, forestry, animal husbandry,fisheries irrigation, rural development and village and cottage industry from Rs. 45,924.70 crore to Rs. 45,523.02 crore (ie from 54.92% to 23.62% of the total public sector outlay). But in spite of the decline in agricultural outaly, rural development culd have been quickened if only there had been more investment in human resources and human developmen. Local resource mobilization with local planning seems to be a promising vehicle for promoting rural development and alleviating poverty.

Local resource mobilization and substitution of human capital as well as physical capital is in conformity with the experience of some of the Scandinaviancountriesand Japan in this context. Theyhave been able to substitute the scarce resources with resource mobilizaton at the local level in rural and agricultural sectorsin particular. Such local resources cannot flow to higher levels but can improve productivity at the local level. This resource augmenting effect has the advatage of accelerating agricultural growth.

In such an effort, equity will have to be given special consideration. The disadvantaged population has to be seen not in therole ofobjects of participation but they are to be integrated as the subjects ofoperation. There should be also anb organizational structure which promotes the effective participation of the disadvantagedpopulation. The emergence of local bodies with elected representatives, one hopes, will make it possible to privide thisinfrastructure.

There should be sound planning at the three levels of District Panchayats, Panchayat Samithis and Village Panchayats.

In the light of the experience and achievements of the revised 20-Point Programme 1982 and the emerging new socio-economic problems during the Seventh Plan (1985-90) the programmes were restructured in 1986 with the directions given by the then Prime Minister Shri Rajiv Gandhi which was popularly known as 20-Point Programme 1986. The restructured programmes came into effect from 1 April 1987 along with Annual Plan of 1987-88. Briefly, the programmes are as under:

— Attack on Rural Poverty: (i) ensure that poverty alleviation programmes reach all the poor in every village; (ii) dovetail wage employment programmes with programmes for area development and human resource development and create national and community assets like school buildings, roads, tanks, fuel and fodder reserves; (iii) correlate the various rural development productivity and production-expand rural employment; (iv) promote handlooms, handicrafts, village and small industries and improve skills for self-employment; and (v) Revitalise Panchayats, cooperatives and local bodies.

— Strategy for Rain-fed Agriculture: (i) improve the technology for conserving moisture and ensure better management of land and water resources; (ii) develop and distribute appropriate and improved seeds; and (iii) reduce vulnerability to drought through suitable changes in droughtprone areas and drought-relief programmes.

— Better use of Irrigation Water: (i) Develop the catchment areas and improve drainage in basins and deltas; (ii) improve irrigation management in command areas; (iii) prevent water logging, salinity and wasteful use; and (iv) coordinate the use of surface and ground water.

— Bigger Harvests: (i) revolutionise rice production in the eastern region and other areas of low productivity; (ii) achieve self-reliance in edible oils; (iii) secure greater production of pulses; (iv) intensify the cultivation of fruits and vegetables; (v) augment facilities for modern storage, processing and marketing of agricultural produce; (vi) help livestock and dairy framers to increase productivity; and (vii) develop fish farming and sea fishing.

— Enfrocement of Land Reforms: (i) complete compilation of land records; (ii) implement agricultural land ceilings; and (iii) distribute surplus land to the landless.

— Special Programmes for Rural Labour: (i) enforce minimum wages for unorganised labour in agriculture and industry, (ii) fully implement laws abolishing bonded labour; and (iii) involve voluntary agencies in prigrammes for the rehabilitation of bonded labour.

— Clean Drinking Water: (i) provide safe water all villages; (ii) assist local communities to maintain the sources of such water supply in good condition; (iii) pay special attention to water supply for SCs and STs.

— Health for All: (i)Improve the quality of primary health care; (ii) fight leprosy, TB malaria, goitre, blindness and other major diseases; (iii) provide immunisation for all infants and children; (iv) improve sanitation facilities in rural areas, particularly for women; and (v) pay special attention to programmes for the rehabilitation of the handicapped.

— Two Child Norm: (i) bring about voluntary acceptance ofthe two child norm; (ii) promote responsible parenthood; (iii) reduce infant mortality; and (iv) expand maternity and child care facilities.

— Expansion of Education: (i) universalise elementary education with special emphasis on girls' education; (ii) improve the content of education at all levels; (iii) promote non-formal education and functional literacy programmes, including promotion of skills; (iv) stimulate adult literacy programmes, with the participation of students and voluntary agencies; and

(v) emphasis on national integration and social and moral values and instil pride in our heritage.

— Justice to Scheduled Castes and Scheduled Tribes: (i) ensure compliance with the constitutional provisions and laws for the SCs and STs; (ii) ensure possession of land allotted to SCs and STs; (iii) revitalise the land allotment programme; ()iv) organise and assist special coaching programmes to immprove educational standards, (v) eradicate scavenging and undertake special programmes for the rehabilitation of Safai Karamcharis; (vi) provide better direction and adequate funds for the special component programmes; (vii) pursue programmes for the fuller integration of SCs and STs with the rest of the society; and (viii) ensure the rehabilitation of tribals displaced from their habitat.

— Equality for Women: (i) raise the status of women; (ii) enhance awareness of the problems of women; (iii) create mass consciousness about women's rights; (iv) implement a national programme of training and employment for women; (v) enable women to participate with equality in socio-economic development and nation-building; and (vi) rouse public opinion against dowry and ensure effective implementation of anti-dowry legislation.

— New Opportunities for Youth: (i) enlarge opportunities for youth in sports, adventure and cultural activities; (ii) promote physical fitness; (iii) involve youth on a massive scale in projects of national development such as the cleaning of the Ganga, the conservation and enrichment of the environment and mass education; (iv) identify outstanding young persons in all fields to encourage and develop their talents; (v) involve youth in temper; (vi) expand the network of Nehru Yuvak

Kendras; (vii) strengthen the National Service Scheme and the National Cadet Corps; and (viii) encourage voluntary agencies working for the welfare of rural youth.

— Housing for the People: (i) make available house sites to the rural poor; (ii) expand programmes of house construction; (iii) lay special emphasis on construction of houses for SCs and STs; and (iv) develop low cost building materials.

— Improvement of Slums: (i) restrict the growth of slums; (ii) provide basic facilities in existing slum areas; and (iii) encourage planned house building in urban areas.

— New Strategy for Forestry: (i) grow more trees and raise more firest, with the full involvement of the people; (ii) protect the traditional rights of tribal populations and local communities of access to fuel wood and forest produce; (iii) reclaim wastelands for productive use; and (iv) plant appropriate vegetation in hilly, desert and coastal areas.

— Protection of the Environment: (i) enhance public awareness of the dangers of environmental degradation; (ii) mobilise popular support for environmental protection; (iii) promote recognition that enduring development demands preservation of the ecology; and (iv) ensure judicious site selection for projects and proper choice of technology.

— Concern for the Consumers: (i) bring essential consumption goods within easy reach of the poor; (ii) build a consumer protection movements; (iii) restructure the distribution system so that subsidies reach the most needy; and (iv) strengthen the public distribution system.

— Energy for the Villages: (i) expand the supply of electricity for productive use in the villages; (ii) develop alternative sources of energy, particularly biogas; and (iii) promote integrated area specific programmes for rural energy.

— A Responsive Administration: (i) simplify procedures; (ii) delegate authority; (iii) enforce accountablility; (iv) evolve monitoring systems from block to national level; and (v) attend promptly and sympatherically to public grievances.

While the restructured 20-Point Programme renewed the nation's commitment to eradicate poverty, it laid balanced emphasis on how to raise overall procductivity, reduce income inequalties and remove social and economic disparities so that the ultimate fruits of development resulted in improvement of quality of life of human environment. The coverage of the programme was broadened to bring within its ambit a number of lmajor areas of social concern for fulfiling not only the 'basic needs' like adeauate provison of food, clean drinking water, housing and health facilities, it laid more emphasis on human dignity and individual rights by encouraging 'responsible' parenthood, equality for women, opportunities for the youth, rights of consumers, justice to scheduled castes and scheduled tribes, etc. The inherent philosophy behind the restructured programme was that the development has no real meaning without human dignity and individual rights.

The Government was not content with mere re-establishment of law and order. It was keen that the new sense of national purpose should be harnessed to a speedier promotion of economic growth and social justice. On 1 July, 1975, the Prime Minister announced in a nationwide broadcast a "Twenty-Point Economic Programme" designed to achieve speedy development and to remove many of the evil practices which and persisted all these years, including bonded labour and rural indebtedness. It gave a further fillip to the official drive to contain inflation and root out black money. The programme was acclaimed by all sections of the people notably farmers and landless workers, industrial workers, representatives of trade and industry, and students and teachers. This meant:

— Continuance of steps to bring down prices of essential commodities. Streamlined production, procurement and distribution of essential commodities. Strict economy in government expenditure.

— Implementation of agricultural land ceilings and speedier distribution of surplus land compilation of land records.

— Stepping up of provision of house sites for landless and weaker sections.

— Bonded labour, wherever it exists, will be declared illegal.

— Plan for liquidation of rural indebtedness. Legislation for moratorium on recovery of debt from landless labourers, small farmers and artisans.

— Review of laws on minimum agricultural wages.

— Five million more hectares to be brought under irrigation. National programme for use of underground water.

— An accelerated power programme. Super thermal stations under central control.

— New development plan for development of handloom sector.

— Improvement in quality and supply of people's cloth.

— Socialisation of urban and urbanisable land. Ceiling on ownership and possession of vacant land and on plinth area of new dwelling units.

— Special squads for valuation of conspicuous construction and prevention of tax evasion. Summary trails and deterrent punishment of economic offenders.

— Special legislation for confiscation of smugglers' properties.

— Liberalisation of investment procedures. Action against misuse of import licences.

— New schemes for workers' association of industry.

— National permit schemes for road transport.

— Income Tax relief to middle class; exemption limit placed at Rs. 8,000.

— Essential commodities at controlled prices to students in hostels.

— Books and stationery at contolled prices.

— New apprenticeship scheme to enlarge employment and training, especially of weaker sections.

Farm agencies to adopt 50,000 families—transfer of technology

Involvement of all the 860 institutions and agencies of the Indian Council of Agricultural Research (ICAR), agricultural universities and voluntary agencies for the transfer of farm techniques to the field level with adoption of 50,000 agricultural families in the programme, has been recommended by the ICAE national workshop on transfer of technology programme for rural development.

The three-day workshop has also decided to prepare a "lab to land operational manual" providing information on all available technologies, besides embarking upona continuous monitoring and evaluation of the implementation of the programme for making midcourse corrections. Such a manual will pay special attention to the small and marginal farmers and provide viable technology to them.

The workshop has decided that while ICAR and its agencies and the agricultural universities and their centres should adopt 20,000 farmers each, the voluntary organisations and affiliated agricultural college could be entrusted with the task of adopting 10,000 families.

The workshop felt that in selecting centres, preference should be given to institutions already involved in agricultural development and the selection of blocks, villages, farm families should also be preferably from the intensive agricultural development blocks already identified.

The approach for the transfer of technology should be on a cluster-village basis and proximity of the implementing agency should also be borne in mind for effective supervision.

Another important recommendation of the workshop was that related programmes for farm youth, farm women and children should be taken up simultaneously. It also strongly recommended creation of suitable marketing infrastructure and facilities well in advance to match the anticipated increased production.

The workshop recommended organisation of agricultural exhibitions at national, State, institute and university levels, during the national extension fortnight celebrations—inter-State and inter-regional exchanges, lectures by farm-professors organisation of debates and discussions special programmes and features on the radio, television, press and extension lectures should be taken up during the fortnight, it said.

Monitoring and evaluation

The departments/ministries concerned on the subject of 20-Point Programme, 1986 set the annual targets in consultation with the states and the Department of Programme Implementation (DPI). DPI monitors the implementation of the 20-Point Programme. The management information system developed by this Department for implementation of the programmes consists of (i) Monthly Progress Report; (ii) Capsule Report; (iii) Half Yearly Progress Report; and (iv) Annual Report.

Under 20-Point Programme-1986, there are 119 items identified for monitoring. Of these, 54 are monitored on an evaluatory basis and 65 items are retained for physical targetting/monitoring. Again of the 65 items identified for quantitative assessment, 28 items have been identified for monitoring on a monthly basis. Only 19 items, out of the 28 items of the Monthly Report, are taken for the purpose of ranking. The Half Yearly Report covers majority of the items of 20-Point Programme indicating qualitative performance.

A three-tier system of monitoring has been established in the states/UTs, as follows: (a) at the agency level which are entrusted with the execution of the programmes in the field level; (b) at the state level which provides infrastructure and direction for programme execution; and (c) at the Central Government level not only by the sectoral ministries and departments but also by the Department of Programme Implementation under the Ministry of Planning and Programme Implementation, which oversees the monitoring and evaluation system on a contiuous basis and reports to the Cabinet Secretriat and the Prime Minister's Office.

The concern for human poverty and its eradication to improve human environment have been the central focus of our development planning in the country since the inception of the planing era. Various schemes have been formulated and implemented with the sole objective of removing poverty and thereby increasing the quality of life of the people in the lower ranks of population. The explicit manifestation of the government's concern for poverty alleviation got its expression when the first 20-Point Programme was launched on 1 July 1975 under the connotation of *Ganibi Hatao* which was conceived by the late Prime Minister Smt Indira Gandhi. This programme was implemented with a pragmatic success during 1975-76 and 1976-77 Annual Plans. The Sixth Five Year Plan (1980-85)) incorporated these programmes as guiding factors in the planning process. Taking the past experience, the original 20-Point Programme was further re-defined, revitalized and announced to the Nation on 14 January 1982.

Objectives

Increase irrigation potential, develop and dissemiinate technologies and imputs for dry land agriculture; (ii) Make special efforts to increase production of pulses and vegetable oilseeds;

Strengthen and expand coverage of integrated rural development and national rural employment programmes; (iv) Implement agricultural land ceilings, distribute surplus land and complete compilation of land records by removing all administrative and legal obstacles; (v) Review and effectively enforce minimum wages for agricultural labour; (vi) Rehabilitate bonded labour; (vii) Accelerate programmes for the development of scheduled castes and scheduled tribes; (viii) Supply drinking water to all problem villages; (ix) Allot house sites to rural families who are without them and expand programmes for construction assistance to them; (x) Improve the environment of slums, implement programmes of house building for economically weaker sections and take measures to arrest unwarranted increase in land prices; (xi) Maximise power generation, improve the functioning of electricity authorities and electrify all villages; (xii) Pursue vigorously programmes of afforestation social and farm forestry and the development of bio-gas and other alternative energy sources; (xiii) Promote family planning on a voluntary basis as a people's movement; (xiv) Substantially augment universal primary health care facilities and control of leprosy, TB and blindness; (xv) Accelerate programmes of welfare for women and children and nutrition programmes for pregnant women, nursing mothers and children, specially in tribal hill and backward areas; (xvi) Spread universal elementary education for the age group 6-14 with special emphasis on girls and simultaneously involve students and voluntary agencies in programmes for the removal of adult illiteracy; (xvii) Expand the public distribution system through more fair price shops, including mobile shops in far flung areas and shops, to cater to industrial workers, students' hostels, and make available to students textbooks and exercise books on a priority basis and to promote a strong consumer protection movement; (xviii) Liberalise investment procedures and streamline industrial policies to ensure timely completion of projects. Give handicrafts, handlooms, small and village industries all facilities to grow and to update their technology; (xix) Continue strict action against smugglers, hoarders and tax evaders and tax evaders and check black money; and (xx) Improve the working of the public enterprises by increasing efficiency, capacity utilisation and the generation of internal sources.

Various programmes were formulated to achieve the above objectives focussing mostly on the critical socio-economic constraints on development. The existence of human poverty was considered the single most adverse constraints to human development. Therefore, breaking the vicious circle of poverty which was both the cause and the effect of under development in the country was central to the formulation of 20-Point Programme. The Sixth Five Year Plan was designed taking note of the micro-objectives of 20-Point Programme in the critical sectors which were accorded high priority in the planning process. The emphasis on agricultural productivity, rural employment, provision of safe drinking water, allotment of houses sites to the rural families, improvement of slums, voluntary family planning, provision of basic health care, concern for environmental degradation, spread of elementary education, accelerating welfare programmes for the women and children were the most positive features of the revised 20-Point Programme which were spelt out keeping in view the basic objective of the development planning that the fruits of planning mustensure the 'basic needs' of human beings if development process is at all to be sustainable.

While the various evaluation reports indicate different positive impacts, the major impact of the 20-Point Programme in the country was the re—distribution of productive assets in favour of the less privileged who are the backbone of the economy. From the point of view of a sustainable growth, these programmes not only improve the productivity in the rural sector but also increased the overal quality of life in the villages to a perceptible degree.

Community initiatives & people's participation

It is evident from the above discussion that the Panchayats have been denied the possibility of carrying out participatory planning for local development at the grass roots level. This vacuum has been filled by the voluntary efforts of the people with the participation of intellectuals and voluntary network organizations like the Kerala Sastra Sahitya Parishad, Bharat Vigyan Samithi. The results of their efforts have been remarkable. In the field of literacy, the "Erankulam model" is acclaimed across the world and replicated elsewhere in India. The alphabet literacy has provided a sound base for a mass initiative in the field of environment protection, gender equality and women's empowerment. Thus social development in Kerala has been the contribution of an awakened and vigilant public. Majumdar (1995) rightly observed that "The enlightened and politically conscious electorate in Kerala closely monitors the functioning of schools, including those in the rural areas. Here, cases of shirking on the part of teachers evoke strong collection protest (e.g. many such cases are immediately publicised through posters in public places), and as a corollary, elicit appropriate policy responses.

The expansion of literacy has given a sound base for participatory planning which has successfully been operationalised in Kalliasseri Panchayat in Kannur district of the State.

The Community Development Society (CDS), with its thrift and credit activities, has improved the lot of poor women in urban Kerala. The Alappuzha CDS is an example, where "poor women have mobilized up to Rs. 37 lakh from their own savings. In two years, the Alappuzha CDS has generated more than 4,000 jobs ensuring 100 per cent loan recovery and repayment to banks as on date". Due to this exemplary work, the Alappuzha model has received "We the People Award" in 1994 from the United Nations.

Although Kerala could not provide a successful

model for participatory planning through Panchayats due to political instability, its people, with the help of dedicated voluntary organizations have offered one. The other States could benefit from its success stories in participatory planning.

Development is the primary concern and responsibility of the people. They must prepare the plan and implement the same. This is much more true with the introduction of Panchayati Raj. The voluntary organizations may also be actively involved in this task. People are the primary concern. It is their confidence and credibility that needs to be obtained. It is mutual trust between government and the people that will repose faith in each other. There are three basic principles of people-centred development. First, sovereignty resides with the people. Second, to exercise their sovereignty and assume responsibility for their own development and that of their communities, people must control their own resources, have access to relevant information, and have the means to hold the officials of government and voluntary organizations accountable. Third, those who would assist people with their development must recognize that it is they who are participating in support of the people's agenda, not vice-versa. The value of the outsider's contribution will be measured in terms of the enhanced capacity of the people to determine their own future.

The Gandhian model of development requires active involvement and participation of man building his own "destiny". This is possible if some of us belonging to the so-called rich and middle class voluntarily, instead of dfrifting toward consumerism, are willing to sacrifice and share our pleasures in the interests of the downtrodden of our society. For rural India, time is running out and it must adopt strategies and methods to transform the socio-economic life of people to suit Indian ingenuity and culture. Integrated development sets forth a strategy of working with rural people—a strategy, in which participation by all is both the means and end itself.

In sum, the real wealth of a country lies in "human capital" and if you create conditions where human capital can flourish without being squashed by government controls, you can beat the rest of the countries of the Ninth Plan has to be very positive in building up "social capital" and infrastructure. Our social achievements are not outstanding despite our fifty years of Independence. Our literacy rate is 52 per cent; infant mortality 74 per thousand; access to sanitation is available to only 16 per cent of the people. Though life expectancy has gone up to 62, the fertility rate is still 3.3 which would double India's population in the next century. Just as the proof of the pudding is in the eating, similarly the success of the Ninth Plan will depend on as to how far it has raised "human capotal" of India.

We have to shift the paradigm of development from a right centred-economy to a duty motivated economy, from self-centredness to the love of our fellowmen, if we want to succeed in our planned development of rural society.

Participatory planning

We have seen that Panchayats in Kerala have not become a viable and pulsating institution for ensuring participatory planning. The prime mover in this sphere has been the voluntary sector, But after the 73rd Constitutional Amendment which, among other things, has ensured regular elections to the Panchayats and reservation of seats as well as of posts of Chairpersons for the weaker sections at all the tiers, they have to assume this role. The elections to these institutions were also held last year.

The People's Campaign for the formulation of the Ninth Plan has also been launched in the State for making decentralized Planning the key input in preparing the State Plan. All these efforts on the part of the State government are in the right direction. But the main question is whether the Panchayats have really emerged as institutions of self-government (as envisaged in Article 243 G of the Constitution) to help materialize participatory planning. As mentioned earlier, the two important dimensions of the people's participation are: who are the people and how would the participation occur. The answer to the first question is given by M.A. Oommen (1991) while discussing the formulation of a methodology for district planning with people's participation in Kannur district where he says, by people we mean those below the poverty line. The poor people, including other marginalized sections of society, have been statutorily given berth in Panchayats. The second question is also answered by constituting the Panchayats in the State.

But the most important question regarding realization of the objective of participatory planning is whether people enjoy autonomy in their actions. In other words, whether the various provisions of the State Panchayat Act establish Panchayats as an Institution of Self-government (ISG), i.e. whether they have institutional existence, institutional capacity and financial viability. Therefore, the question discussed in this part of the paper is whether the various provisions of the Kerala Panchayat Act enable Panchayats to usher in participatory planning. And if not, what amendments need to be made.

Financial autonomy

Autonomy of people's actions which is the basis for participatory planning can only be operationalized if Panchayats enjoy financial autonomy. Let us examine the provisions of the Kerala Panchayat Raj Act to see to what extent they obstruct the exercise of this autonomy and how financial autonomy can be provided to them.

— Imposition of particular tax or levy or cess should be compulsory. If a tax is not compulsory, it could not be an effective instrument in the hands of the Panchayats to mobilise finance. For example, house tax is compulsory in Andhra Pradesh and Haryana and optional in Uttar Pradesh. Because of its mandatory nature, it has yielded more finance in Andhra Pradesh and Haryana than in Uttar Pradesh. In the Kerala Panchayati Raj Act, powers to collect fixed fees (Section 198), building tax, profession tax, advertisement tax and entertainment tax (Section 200) are not mandatory for exercise by the Panchayats. Hence, the should be made as such.

— Under the Act, rates of the cess shall be governed the rules made by the government. After repealing this provision, the Panchayats should be empowered to decide the rate of a particular cess.

— The scope for imposing taxes should also be enlarged. In this regard, Panchayats should be empowered to auction river sand, levy fee on quarrying and for pumping water from canals etc.

— A provision should also be made in the Act that if a lower tier of Panchayat is unable to perform the assigned functions, the next higher tier shall examine the problem and help it out. Besides, helping out the lower tier of Panchayat, this will also establish an organic link between the different tiers. One of the important features of the Gujarat Panchayat (TP) shall provide resources to enable it to perform its functions effectively (Section 204).

— The Karnataka Panchayat Act provides for

arrangement of grant for the GP under which a grant of Rs. 1 lakh is to be provided by the State government. This amount shall be used to meet electricity charges, maintenance of water supply scheme, etc. of the GP (Section 208). No other State has made this kind of a provision for GPs, Kerala should also have such a provision in its Panchayat Act.

— There must be a separate head for Panchayats in the State budget. This head should include share from tax and non-tax revenue, grant-in-aid and resources allocated to Panchayats for performing agency functions.

— As per Section 214 (7) of the Act, the Village Panchayats and Block Panchayats shall submit their budgets to the Panchayat, which along with its budget submit them to the government. This is against the letter and spirit of local government. Budgets passed by the VPs should go the BP which after consolidating them should submit them to the DP. The DP, instead of sending them to the government, should submit the budget of this whole rular area to the District Planning Committee which, after consolidating the plans of rural and urban areas should submit it to the State government.

— In order to examine and scrutinize the accounts of the Panchayats, West Bengal has constituted a District Council comprising the largest recognized political party in the opposition its Chairperson, one Vice-Chairperson and five other members to be elected by the members of the DP and three government officers nominated by the government. A similar provision may also be adopted by Kerala for financial discipline of the Panchayats.

— The MPs' Local Area Development Scheme which is implemented by Distict Collectors may be implemented through Panchayats and municipalities, because items of works of this scheme are almost similar to the XI Schedule of the Constitution. If this is done, it will not only help in according financial autonomy to the local government but also lessen spatial gaps in various social infrastructures. When this scheme was introduced in Parliament, only the left parties objected to it on the plea that it went against the spirit of decentralization. In Kerala, where the same parties are now in power, they should how the political Panchayats and the municipalities.

Constitution and composition of panchayats

Not giving membership to MPs and MLAs in Panchayats, not tampering with the VP and Block Panchayats (BPs) boundaries for the membership of the BPs and the District Panchayat, (DP) respectively and making the Chairpersons of the lower tier members of the immediate upper tier for establishing an organic link among them are welcome features of the State Act, which should also be emulated by other States. But there are certain features of the Act which need to be amended as they are against the spirit of the Central Act and participatory planning. These are:

— In Chapter II of the Act, reorganization of the boundaries of the wards of Panchayats has been vested in the State government, which is against the provisions of Articles 243 k and 243 O of the Constitution. All functions pertaining to the delimitation of boundaries, including disputes between or among Panchayats, should be performed by the State Election Commission.

— A provision for reservation of OBCs should also be made in the Act to enable them to participate effectively in decentralized governance.

— The election of the Chairperson of the VP should be made direct as is the case in most States. In this way, the Chairperson will be able to draw authority from the people. Besides making Chairpersons accountable to the people, this will also strengthen the institution of the GS.

— To provide more space for weaker sections to participate in planning and development, the reservation for SCs, STs, OBCs and women should be extended to include the post of Vice-Chairperson of different tiers. At present, Punjab is the only State where such a provision has been made at the intermediate and apex tiers. Kerala may do well to go one step further and provide reservation for these sections at all tiers of the Panchayats.

— As per Section 151 of the Act, if the government is satisfied that a Panchayat at any level cannot be constituted for certain reasons, like failure to elect the majority of the members, it can appoint an Administrative Committee consisting of at least the elected members and a President and Vice-President, or appoint a special officer for period not exceeding six months. This provision is against the spirit of the Constitution. If such an eventuality arises, only the elected representatives should govern the Panchayats for a specified period and not a special officer. Therefore, the provision of a special officer provided in this section should be deleted.

Functional autonomy

Devolving of adequate and clear-cut functions and powers to the Panchayats is very important for enabling them to function in a free environment. Let us examine the scope of Kerala Panchayat Raj Act (KPRA) in this regard.

— Under Section 164 (2), a provision has been made for constituting a Ward Committee for each constituency with the purpose of informing the VP on the needs of the constituency. But the GS will also be held at the ward level only, which among others, will list out its needs as is also envisaged as the role of the Ward Committee. The VP may also constitute a vigilance Committee as suggested earlier in this paper. Keeping these provisions in view, constitution of the Ward Committee is dispensable.

— The District panchayats, Block Panchayats and Village Panchayats shall perform their functions under the financial and technical guidance of the State government [Sections 166 (2), 172 (2) 173 (2)]. This is wrong in principle and operationally difficult as it does not put Panchayats on a firm foundation. Through provisions of this nature, the government can meddle with the functioning of the democratically elected institutions and deprive the people of freedom of action which is essential for participatory planing.

  These provisions in the State Act may have to be suitably amended so that the VP takes help from the BP which, in turn, takes help from the DP and the DP from the State government, if it is required. The State may be benefited from the Panchayati Raj Acts of States like Gujarat, Assam, Manipur and Madhaya Pradesh which have enabling provisions for consultation among the three tires without much intervention from the State.

— Functions to be performed by different tiers of Panchayats have been listed in Schedules 3,4 and 5 of the Act. Looking at their distribution among the three tiers, an hour glass picture emerges, because they have been concentrated either at the lowest level or at the apex. This shows that in deciding the distribution, proper thought has not been given. For example, functions relating to education do not figure in the list for the BP, which thus emerges as a weak tier of the PR system and, therefore, does not provide sufficient scope for its members to play a role in participatory planning.

While participating in the Conference of Chief Ministers on basic minimum services 4-5, July, 1996 in Delhi, the Chief Minister of Kerala mentioned that less than one per cent of the total habitations in the State were fully covered as regards the availability of safe drinking water against the national coverage of 57 per cent. Shortage of clean drinking water is an important reason for the high morbidity in the State. This is one of the basic needs and could be handled effectively at Panchayat level. But very little responsibility to this basic necessity has been devolved to the Panchayats. It is suggested that in order to conserve water resources, construction of check dams in the rivers should be entrusted to the Panchayats. If this function is given lock stock and barrel to the Panchayats, it being a basic requirement, will enthuse the people to participate in water management.

— In inter-tier allocation of functions, the cardinal principle that what can be undertaken at a particular level should be entrusted to that level alone has been kept in mind. However, ample scope for improving the functional relationship between the three tiers is still there. Significantly, whatever functions have been allocated to the Panchayats in accordance with this principle have been taken away by Section 283, according to which the government may alter, amend or add to any of the entries made in the functions of the Panchayats. Hence this section should be repealed.

— To fully realize economic development and social justice, other functions like police powers and judicial powers should also be given to the Panchayats. Bihar, West Bengal, Punjab and Uttar Pradesh are the States which have given judicial functions to institutions at the grass roots level. Recently, the Madhya Pradesh State Assembly has also passed a legislation for constituting Gram Nyayalayas to administer justice in rural areas. The Karnataka government also proposes to introduce an amendment to the State's Panchayat Act in the coming session of the Assembly for setting up Nyaya Panchayats. The kerala Panchayat Raj Act does not make provision for constituting Nyayalaya at grass roots levels for dispensing justice to the people. It is, therefore, suggested that police and judicial functions should be given to the Panchayats for meaningful decentralization

Functional autonomy has not been given to the Panchayats, because provisions such as the schemes being contingent on the availability of resources and placing of performance of vital functions under the supervision and guidance of the government have circumscribed the role of participatory planning through the institutions. For ushering in an era of participatory planning for Panchayats, the State government should amend all the Acts pertaining to the subjects in the XIth Schedule of the Central Act, take out all relevant portions from the existing Subjects Acts and incorporate them in the Panchayat Act through an amendment by the State legislature.

Administrative autonomy

For enabling the people to participate effectively in planning and development of their areas through Panchayats, it is indispensable that these bodies should have their own officials. But this has not been provided for in the Kerala Panchayat Act.

— The secretaries of all the three tiers will be the government employees (Section 179) under the State Act. The power of transferring these employees is also vested in the government or in a prescribed authority if a resolution to that effect has been passed by the Panchayat by a simple majority. However, action on this resolution is not mandatory on the part of the government. This provision is objectionable, because this does not entail autonomy of the people in their actions. What is the rationale behind insisting on a simple majority for a resolution for transferring an official? It is practised at the State and the Central levels? Hence this provision may have to be repealed.

— The Chairpersons of the Panchayats have been empowered to exercise supervision and control over the officials of the Panchayats and prepare their confidential reports (Section 156 (4) (b). It is a welcome feature of the Act. But provisions in the Kerala Munidipal Act [Section 14 (3) (b)] which say that Chairpersons prepare the confidential report of the Secretary as well as review the confidential reports prepared by the Secretaries in respect of their employees should also be made applicable to the Panchayats.

— An enabling provision for constituting a separate Service or Cadre [Section 179 (3)] has been made in the Act. Other States which have some such provisions are Karnataka [Section 196 (5) and Punjab

(Section 26). But the provision in the Kerala Act is not substantial in nature as it has not been clearly specified as has been done in the Gujarat Panchayati Raj Act. The provision under Section 179 (3) of the KPRA must be operationalized at once so that the Panchayats have their own officers and employees. Kerala may be benefited from Gujarat and Rajasthan Panchayati Raj Acts in which provisions for Panchayat cadre have already been incorporated. Under the Gujarat Panchayati Raj Act, there will be three cadres of Panchayat employees, namely the District cadre, the Taluk cadre and the Local cadre [Section 227 (3)]. For this purpose, a Gujarat Panchayat Service Selection Board shall be constituted. Besides this Board, a District Panchayat Service Selection Committee shall also be constituted at the district-level to recruit the primary education staff (Section 236). In Rajasthan, a provision for establishing a District Establishment Committee under the chairpersonship of the President of the ZP has been made. This Committee shall make selections for the posts in different grades and categories for the Panchayats, prepare lists of the persons for promotion and deal with disciplinary matters affecting the officers and employee except officers of the State cadre.

Actually, a permanent solution of the cadre problem is to amend the Constitution, because the Panchayats after becoming local government must have their own employees as the State and the Centre have as per part XIV of the Constitution. But to begin with, the State government must invoke immediately the enabling provisions in the Panchayat Act.

Modern planning

Whether it is fully realized or not, the Ninth Plan planning represents a new age planning of an age of management culture, economic restructuring, resource scarcity, economy, value for investment, global competition, MNCs, mega investments, free trade, intellectual property rights, R & D, productivity, quality, efficiency, hardware and software of production, human capital, strategic planning, economic vision, government-private sector partnership, value by results, international capital, regional economic groupings, delicensing, decentralization, lean taxation, FDI, foreign borrowings, JVs, market pricing, opening of the economies, public-private sector parity or equality, fiscal discipline, public-orientation, deregulations, budgetary imbalances, de-nationalisation, corporate takeovers, subsidy-cuts, commercialization of agriculture and free trade in agricultural goods, non-farm enterprises in rural areas, entrepreneurship, innovations, paid lunches, cutting down free rides, user-charges, gender equality and empowerment of women, and soon.

Break from the past: In spite of its not insignificant achievements, the bane of Indian planning has been poor implementation and results, viz operational shortcomings and 'targetism'. The Ninth Plan should and ought to make a break from it, to justify its nearly Rs. 1 crore investiment. It must have multiple effect, without which it is bad planning, though the plans do not work out the multipliers. The plan has to learn a leaf or two from corporate planning, particularly of MNCs which mean business of every dollar of investment. Not that the Plan should be devoid of human concerns and values, which it or for that matter any public planning anywhere should be responsive to, given the concern of planning with the have-nots. That is, the results of the planning need be measured not only, by the hard facts of growth rate but also by the light and laughter in the lives of the common people, visible to the naked eye. Otherwise, the purpose of the whole planning exercise would be much lost.

Meeting the challenge: All said and done, the fact should be brought home to the planners in the Ninth Plan that it requires a lot of suffering and sacrifice to make the Plan operative with so much investment and it should yield commensurate returns in health, education, employment, social infrastructure, economic overheads, employment, enterprises, etc. for which the Plan is intended. India is one of the most poverty-ridden and low income countries. Our per capita income is not even $ 400 per annum. Millions and millions of people's daily concerns water, sanitation, medical aid, food and employment. Accordingly, the new age planning consists of making plan investments go as far as possible or maximum yielding. Planning must make the deserts bloom, not allow the forests to vanish so to say. If not, it is not proper planning.

Whether the plan size is optimal, suboptimal or overoptimal is irrelevant in the context of the plan. From plan-to-plan, planning efforts anyhow need to be raised. Considering This the plan is not at all oversized, considering the magnitude of the problems facing the economy and the efforts needed to overcome them. It is a different thing if the nation opts for a soft and small Ninth Plan. At no time, the plans had escaped the label of being ambitious and oversized. Notwithstanding plan size, the basic economic problems remain intact, if the poverty-line population increasing recently to 37 per cent is any indication.

An opportune time: Only, the Ninth Plan should be a new age planning or plan of operational efficiency, economy, efficiency, discipline, human and grass roots development, competitive, forward looking, co-ordinating and comprehensive. In addition, it must be time and cost bound. No doubt, it is a tall order of things but it is unavoidable if the Ninth Plan is to spell a success and make a dent into the thousand problems of the economy and the people. We have been lethargic with planning and it is time to be strictly business and management minded about planning and plan and the Ninth Plan is the right and opportune time to commence new age planning, without which it becomes increasingly difficult to sustain planning.

That is the law of diminishing returns which appears to have set in planning, since long, needs to be reversed in the Ninth Plan, failing which zero and even negative marginal productivities may set in for plan investments. There are increasing constraints on plan resources due to which the Ninth Plan should successfully go through its arithmetic of investments and returns in different lines of production and try to realize them for the first time in planning history of the country in tune with the new age stress on returns rather than or just investments. The Ninth Plan, in other words, should incorporate into its functioning strict business principles. The Plan thus should open a new chapter in planning not only in India but also the world over. Planning should assert itself and march ahead in the so-called market ruled economy and dispense its benefits to its large multitudes standing second to none in economy, efficiency and execution. It is the mandate of the populace. There is a national consensus behind planning, particularly the Ninth Plan, which promises to be a plan of action and of the people. It promises to give thrust to the thrust areas. Economy, productivity, returns and people should be the watchwords of new planning to commence with the Ninth Plan. There is no activity commensurate in importance with the Plan that should be No. 1 programmes, as nothing involves such a massive investment and the welfare and happiness of millions and millions of people and their living and natural environment.

One has to harp at length about the need for new planning because of the debris that is being left behind by improper planning, which is downward rather than upward. Rural development, for instance, is a greatly neglected aspect of our planning and the Ninth Plan promises to remove the whole backlog of it including human resource development and women and child development. Great challenges lay ahead of the new planning process.

According to Prof Madhu Dandavate, Deputy Chairman of the Planning Commission, the Ninth Plan accords "the highest priority to generating adequate productive employment, eradication of poverty, focus on agriculture and rural development with emphasis on radical land reforms".

Power—Crucial Infrastructure: Pointing out that the power sector constitutes the most crucial infrastructure both for agriculture and industry, he said that the problems of power must be carefully handled in a co-ordinated fashion with due attention for the proper choice of fuels, the adequacy of their availability, the need to rationalize tariff structure, and to prevent transmission and distribution losses.

In fact, the problem of power may reach crisis proportions in the next few years unless urgent action is taken by every state. The financial, managerial and administrative structue of State Electricity Boards (SEBs) and their policies must be changed dramatically and urgently so that the Electricity Boards can raise tariffs to realistic levels, improve the quality of supply, contain power theft and become financially viable. The Finance Minister, Mr. P. Chidambaram, is of the view that the Central and State laws need to be changed to allow SEBs and private electricity companies to function autonomously subject to independent regulatory authorities.

Agricultural Growth: In respect of sectoral strategies, the document emphasizes that agriculture has a vital place in the economic development of the country as it contributes 29.4 per cent of GDP and employs about 64 per cent of the workforce. There has been a significant improvement in agricultural productivity which has helped in reducing rural poverty. It is noted that capital formation (at 1980-81 prices) in agriculture grew at tha rate of 6.05 per cent during 1989-90 to 1994-95. In the accelerated growth scenario for the Ninth Plan, efforts will need to be made to achieve an agricultural growth rate of 4.5 per cent per annum in contrast with 3.5 per cent growth rate during the Eighth Plan period on an average.

The role of basic inputs in agriculture cannot be underestimated. Timely and adequate availabilty of inputs for agriculture and agriculture-related infrastructure will need to receive special attention. Therefore, regional programmes have to be formulated in such a manner as to ensure provision of inputs to the farmer, particularly in the remote, hilly, backward and tribal areas. Likewise, augmentation of irrigation facilities is necessary to increase the gross cropped areas even under rainfed vonditions and invreasing cropping intensity in agriculture areas and assinging priority ot the completion of ongoing projects—both major and minor irrigation.

Ensuring Credit Flow: Another vital input is rural credit. Greater credit flow will be ensured to meet the investment requirements of the farming community for stepping up the growth of production. The approach paper of the Plan stresses that efforts would be made to ensure timely and adequate availability of credit, particularly to small and marginal farmers and tribal farmers at reasonable rates so as to enable them to make investments necessary for higher production. More importantly, the crop insurance scheme is going to receive a big thrust for providing security to marginal and small farmers in rainfed areas during the Ninth Plan period.

Poverty Estimates : Referring to the controversy over poverty estimates exercise, Prof. Dandavate points out that a group in the Plan panes has smoothed out some 'kinks' in the poverty estimate arising out of the appliation of the Lakadwala Committee methodology. He said that the group has suggested that in assessing rural poverty, the agricultural labourers' consumer price index should be used and for estimating urban poverty, the industrial workers' consumer price index should be untilized for updating the poverty line. It is hoped that the Planning Commission would finally decide on this issue during the final draft of the Plan.

Ninth plan approach

The main thrust of the Ninth Plan has been to evolve a shared vision of and a shared commitment to the national objectives and the development strategy not only in the government at all levels but also among all other economic agents. No development strategy can be successful unless each component of the economy works towards a common goal and purpose with the full realisation of the role that has to be played within an overall structure of responsibilities. Some of the tasks needed in respect of rural development are given below:

— The principal task during the Ninth Plan, therefore, is to build on the Eighth Plan, while tackling the problems that have emerged, particularly in areas such as capital formation in agriculture, social sector, regional disparity, and fiscal deficits. Indian economy is still vulnerable and the operation of a more open economic system has to be tempered by judicious public interventions to ensure that these vulnerabilities are gradually overcome.

— Since the planning is done for the entire nation, the strategies for resource augmentation need to cover not only the government at all levels but also those which would be available to other sections of the people.

— Since not all parts of the country are equally endowed to take advantage of growth opportunities, planned intervention is needed to ensure that large imbalances do not occur .

— The Indian economy still has a large number of its citizens who live in acute poverty both in rural and urban areas. Special employment programmes targeted to these people will continue in the Ninth Plan. Special attention will need to be paid to unorganized labour, particularly the agricultural landless labourer.

— There exist large disparities across the various social groups. The disadvantaged groups include members belonging to Scheduled Castes and Scheduled Tribes, other backward classes and minorities. In addition, women and children and the physically handicapped and disabled are also vulnerable. For these sections of society State intervention is required in order to provide them with adequate opportunities for education and employment in an attempt to involve them productively in the development process.

— It is heartening to note that the Plan has identified people's initiative and participation as a "key element" in the process of development, particularly in improving the effectiveness of development outlays which has been declining over the years. It has also recognized that the role of the government should be to facilitate the process of people's involvement by creating the right type of institutional infrastructure, particularly in rural areas.

The progress on this front so far has not been entirely satisfactory primarily due to the fact that the other tiers of the government were not fully integrated into the development strategy. The Plan also asserts that the process of social mobilization and development of people's initiatives cannot be achieved without the active support and involvement of the political system at all levels. In the Plan, the Panchayati Raj bodies in rural areas will be directly involved in the development process. People's involvement via their elected representatives will be realized through "democratic—decentralization".

— Co-operatives will be rejuvenated to enlist people's active participation in these societies. They will be liberated from tight bureaucratic control. Self-help groups, associations of workers or small producers, etc are other forms of institutions which will be encouraged to actively involve people in planning process and implementation. Government will seek active "partnership" with the voluntary sector in organizing and promoting these institutions.

— Domestic entrepreneurship, which is the backbone of the development process, will be fully encouraged through measures to enhance their competitive strength and to facilitate their growth and efficiency. In particular, the small-scale and village and home industries will be provided the proper environment for growth and diversification.

— While new initiatives are being taken for additional investment, optimum utilization of the existing infrastructure should not be neglected. This needs to be done by technology upgradation, systems improvement and ensuring public utilities function on commercial lines. Most importantly, care should be taken to ensure that in the provision of these services, the rural areas are provided their due share both in terms of magnitude as well as technology suited to their needs.

— In regard to subsidies, emphasis is laid to move to a system of transparent subsidies directed towards specific target-groups in a selective manner.

— The Indian Planning process had always laid emphasis on measures to ensure sustainability of the development process not only in economic terms, but also in terms of social and environmental factors. The Ninth Plan will carry this tradition further and consolidate on the creation of conditions for sustainable development.

Plan formulation–more freedom to States: The first novelty of the Ninth Plan is that the Planning Commission has decided to give more freedom to the State governments in formulating their plans. The Planning Commission has decided that in consultation with the Union Ministry of Finance, it will indicate the probable amount of Central assistance available to each State and the State governments would be left free to determine the size of their plans.

It may be recalled in this context that the earlier practice followed was that the State governments would propose specific size of the States' annual plans. The Planning Commission would scrutinize them in detail and then extract a promise of additional resource mobilization from the States before approving the plan size.

This gave unnecessary credibility to the size of the States' plans. Every state would push the plan size to unrealistically high level hoping that the Planning Commission would provide additional plan assistance. This never happened.

As a result, many States used to reduce their plans by December each year and wide gaps used to emerge between the original plan size and the final actual plan. What is more, the plan size came to be politicized at the State level. Nobody would accept the size of the plan lesser than the previous years' and it had to be necessarily higher at least by 10 per cent.

This kind of politicisation has been removed during the Ninth Five Year Plan period. The Planning Commission indicates the gross and net plan assistance available to each State and leaves the final size of the plan to be determined by the State government depending upon its capacity to raise additional revenue. This is the first change in the process of planning introduced by the Planning Commission during the Ninth Five Year Plan period.

Change in accounting format: The second change is that while determining the Central assistance to the State plans, the financial resources which used to flow from the financial institutions like LIC/NABARD/IDB/GIC plus statutory liquidity ratio (SLR) market borrowings were treated as Central government transfers. Though the Central government has control over the borrowing powers of the State governments, particularly when they are indebted to the Central government, these sources of funds are the prerogative of the State governments.

The State governments are free to raise funds through banks and other financial institutions depending upon the financial viability of the projects and their capacity to service the debt. However the Planning Commission and the Union Ministry of Finance have evolved a unified borrowing policy to protect the interests of poorer States and minimise the adverse impact of public borrowing on the economy. Therefore, these financial institutions were asked to co-ordinate their direct lending to the State governments. In this ways, the Planning Commission used to treat SLR and other such borrowings from the developmental financial institutions as part of Central assistance.

This practice was disliked by States like West Bengal an, therefore, the Planning Commission has now changed the accounting format in such a way as to show institutional finance and SLR borrowing as States' own resources available for plan purpose. This does not change the resource position of the States in any way. But it goes a long way in giving them and they need not be at the mercy of the Central government to raise funds from lending institutions.

Planning process decentralized: Thirdly, for the first time the approach paper recognized the federal nature of the Indian planning system and has devoted a separate chapter explaining how the Planning Commission is going to decentralize not merely plan formaulation but also the entire planning process including monitoring of implementation.

The document recognizes the implications of the far-reaching political change that has taken place in India. From the inception of the planning regime, the Central government used to be formed by a national party which used to dictate terms to the state governments But in the 1996 elections, no national party secured a majority and a number of regional parties have joined hands to form the United Front government at the Centre.

This is an unprecedented change in the political scenario. Consequently, the Planning Commision's thinking had to reflect this changed situation and give more voice to the State governments in the planning process. At the same time, the State governments are made to realize that they have to mobilize adequate additional resources and harmonize their budgets with a view to reducing fiscal imbalance in the economy.

Promoting federalism: Furthermore, the Planning Commission has been persuading the Central ministries to transfer a large number of Centrally-sponsored schemes (CSS) along with the corresponding funds to the State governments so that the Central domination in the development process and priorities of the States is reduced.

For instance, about 1823 Centrally-sponsored schemes with an outlay of Rs. 16,038. 19 crore were being implemented during the Eighth Plan period. The Chief Minister's conference held in July, 1996 expressed the view that the number of CSS should be reduced and transferred to the States. But the Central ministers are reluctant to transfer many schemes. They agreed to transfer the schemes worth Rs. 1,300 crore only.

Therefore, the Planning Commission has taken the initiative and is persuading the Central ministries to transfer more schemes along with the funds to the State governments as per the decision of the NDC which has laid down that CSS outlay sould not exceed one-sixth of total Central assistance.

In 1979-80, 71 CSS were transferred to the states with an outlay of Rs. 2,000 crore. While this is not a new phenomenon as it was done earlier also, it still augurs well for the States autonomy. The only occasion when it was done on a large scale was during the Janata Party rule which again gave prominence to true federal structure in the planning process.

The reconstituted Planning Commission believes that the principal task of planning in the post-reform era in our federal framework is to evolve a shared vision of and a shared commitment to the national objectives and the development strategy not only in the government at all levels but also among all economic agents.

The principal objective of the Ninth Plan is to build on the succsses of the VIII Plan, whike tackling the problems that have emerged, particularly in agriculture, living standard of the poor, infrastructure, social sector, regional disparity and fiscal deficits. The IX Plan will facilitate broadening and deepening the economic reforms process to ensure that the fruits of development reach the backward regions of the country and benefit the poorer sections of the society in a time-bound manner.

Provision of BMSs: The conference of State Chief Ministers held in july 1996 made a commitment to provide seven basic minimum services universally by AD 2000. They are (i) safe drinking water, (ii) access to primary health care, (iii) universal primary education, (iv) public housing assistance for the homeless, (v) extension of the midday meal scheme, (vi) road connectivity to all villages, and (vii) food security through the public distribution system for all families below the poverty line. The IX Plan will attempt to operationalize this commitment.

The approach to the IX Plan outlines a long-term fiscal policy stance indicating methods by which resources of the governments at all levels can be augmented in order to reduce and eventually eliminate the revenue deficit at all levels.

Along with aggregate economic growth, balanced regional development has been an essential component of our development strategy from the inception of planning. since not all regions of the country are well-endowed or equipped to take advantage of the growth objectives provided by the market, planned intervention continues to be essential to ensure reduction in regional imbalances.

Care for the poor: Our society continues to have a sizeable number of members who still suffer from abject poverty and deprivation. A vast majority of them do not get an opportunity to participate in the market economy. They are neither able to contribute nor receive anytying from the market process. Special employment programmes to ensure adequate incomes for these sections of the society will continue to be an integral part of the IX Plan. Fruther, appropriate public policies including skill-endowment to the market economy will be part of the Plan.

Uplift of weaker section: Increasing the welfare of the socially and ecnonmically disadvantaged groups, including the Scheduled Castes, Scheduled Tribes and backward classes as well as minorities, handicapped and disabled and women and children is another objective of the Ninth Plan. Planned State intervention is essentisal in order to provide these groups with adequate opportunities for education and employment to enable them to participate productively in the development process.